The World of
Mummies

The World of
Mummies

From Ötzi to Lenin

ALBERT ZINK

Translation by
Cordula Werschkun

First published in Great Britain in 2014 by
PEN & SWORD ARCHAEOLOGY
an imprint of
Pen and Sword Books Ltd
47 Church Street
Barnsley
South Yorkshire S70 2AS

ISBN 978 1 78346 370 1

Printed and bound in Malta by Gutenberg Press Ltd.

Typeset in Times New Roman by
CHIC GRAPHICS

Pen & Sword Books Ltd incorporates the imprints of
Pen & Sword Archaeology, Atlas, Aviation, Battleground, Discovery,
Family History, History, Maritime, Military, Naval, Politics, Railways,
Select, Social History, Transport, True Crime, and Claymore Press,
Frontline Books, Leo Cooper, Praetorian Press, Remember When,
Seaforth Publishing and Wharncliffe.

For a complete list of Pen and Sword titles please contact
Pen and Sword Books Limited
47 Church Street, Barnsley, South Yorkshire, S70 2AS, England
E-mail: enquiries@pen-and-sword.co.uk
Website: www.pen-and-sword.co.uk

Contents

Introduction..7

How does a mummy come about? The different ways of
   mummification..12

Where is the world do mummies exist? The geographic distribution
   of mummies:
     North America 21
     Central America..22
     South America 22
     Europe..23
     Africa 24
     Asia..24
     Oceania and Australia 25

How do mummies date? The age of mummies..................................28

What do mummies tell us? The scientific study of mummies.............32
     Radiological and endoscopic examinations....................33
     Biochemical and histological procedures 36
     Molecular biological analysis 37

Mummies from different regions of the world 38
     Mummies from South America 38
       Juanita, the Inca mummy from the Andes 45
       Chinchorro mummies, the earliest artificially preserved
        mummies 51

     Mummies from Europe...56
       Ötzi, the man from the ice...60
       The violent death of the man from the ice..................65
       Traces of blood on clothing and equipment 67
       New finds...68

The genes of the iceman 71
Rosalia Lombardo and the Capuchin crypt in Palermo.............74
Church mummies from the crypt in Vác, Hungary 84
Lenin and Evita Perón, modern mummies from our time 92

Mummies from Egypt..96
Tutankhamen, the Golden King...............................101
Ramses III and the Harem's Conspiracy 110

Mummies from Asia 115
Lady Dai, a mummy from the Han Dynasty in China.............121
South Korean mummies, swathed in silk 126

Selected Bibliography...135

Illustration credits 141

Introduction

Mummies possess an incredible power of attraction. We can hardly escape the fascination that emanates from the preserved bodies, even though these are dead people who do not always look a pretty sight. Scientists and experts in all kinds of fields simply jump at the chance to examine mummies. Every year thousands upon thousands of visitors stream into the museums of the world to see exhibitions about or including mummies. Exhibitions dealing exclusively with this topic, as for example the one initiated by the Reiss-Engelhorn museums in Mannheim – *Mummies – The Dream of Eternal Life* – have turned out to be veritable crowd-pullers.

Wherein is this enthusiasm founded, what drives us to engage ourselves with the deceased of times past? One reason is certainly that mummies are able to give an immediate insight into the living conditions of our ancestors, for example their diet, their diseases and much more. After all, these are people who have lived sometimes thousands of years ago and therefore able to provide a genuine picture of cultures long since lost. Moreover, a certain immediacy emerges from the preservation of the soft tissue, such as skin, hair and the internal organs, to still recognisable facial features.

We realise that these are people who once lived and perhaps had to battle the same fears and hardships as us, or also experienced the same joys. Furthermore, mummies confront us too, with our own death, with our transience and with the possibility to preserve the body and thus epitomise the dream of eternal life.

Finally, the particular appeal is also often constituted by the special find circumstances or by the historical and cultural context in which the preserved bodies originate. After all, mummies are frequently a part of cultures in which religious concepts have led to the development of techniques to disrupt the course of nature and to

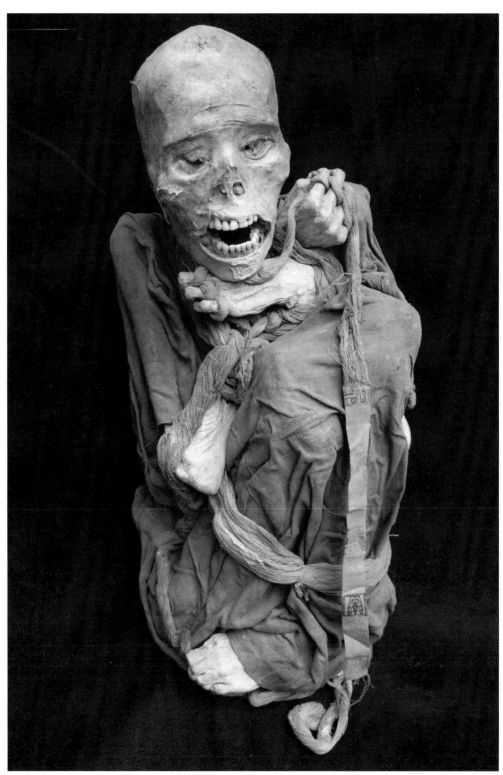

Chachapoya mummy.

preserve the body for a life after death. This is a phenomenon more widely spread than we would at first consider, and that has left its trace to the present day.

We primarily associate Egyptian mummies with the term 'mummies' and, in so doing, first and foremost the famous kings of the pharaonic empires, as for example the young pharaoh Tutankhamen, the 'heretic king' Akhenaten, and the successful warlord and architect Ramses II. Yet also the mummies of high officials and priests, which are found in their dozens in the various museums and collections around the entire globe, have made Egyptian mummies into the embodiment of mummification, and of the wish for physical integrity in the afterlife. The often artfully wrapped mummies of Egypt, and especially the colourfully painted and richly decorated coffins too, with countless grave goods such as jewellery, amulets, vessels and much more, have fascinated researchers and explorers as well as the readers of their accounts, and museum visitors.

Mummies of other cultural spheres are usually far less well-known. An exception is the man from the ice, found in the Öztal Alps (Southern Tirol), who under his nickname 'Ötzi' has likewise attracted great interest. The great age of the glacial mummy (5,300 years), the accidental find circumstances, and also the intense research on his life until his violent death have procured for him an importance both within research and in public perception, not least because most of his clothes and his equipment have survived that enable an entirely new and unique insight into the early Chalcolithic Period of the Alpine region.

Rather less well-known than the man from the ice or the Egyptian mummies, but at least equally impressive, is the mummy of Rosalia Lombardo, which can be found in the catacombs of the Capuchin monastery in Palermo on Sicily. The exceptionally well-preserved body of the young girl, who is also called la bella addormentata (Sleeping Beauty) by the locals, was masterfully embalmed by Alfredo Salafia after her death in 1920. Furthermore, mummies in South America, especially in Peru and Chile, are occasionally reported too. However, probably only very few know that mummies are not restricted to specific regions of the world or to particular cultures but rather represent a world-wide phenomenon. Indeed, mummified

9

Naturally preserved mummy from the Capuchin crypt in Palermo.

human remains are found on all continents and entirely different geographic regions with extremely diverse climatic conditions. These finds range from the members of the Franklin expedition mummified in ice in the north of Canada to the mummies in the highlands and deserts of South America, from the bog bodies in Northern Europe via the different church mummies in the whole of Europe to the Guancha mummies on the Canary Islands, and from the Scythian mummies in Siberia via the Chinese and Korean mummies and Japanese monks to the tattooed heads of the Maori in New Zealand. The date and the manner of mummification vary considerably and heavily depend on the respective environmental conditions.

Therefore the book in hand is not restricted to a few well-known mummies but wishes to provide a comprehensive overview of the mummy phenomenon. Firstly it shall be clarified in which manner mummies come about, where they have been found and to which time they date. Subsequently mummies from all regions of the world are introduced, with particular attention to research results that have been obtained most recently.

1

How does a mummy come about? The different ways of mummification

The normal process after the occurrence of death is the decomposition of a corpse, which by this means is fed again into the natural metabolic cycle. This starts initially with the so-called autolysis, representing an auto-degradation of cells and organic structures by endogenous enzymes. Immediately following are the processes of decay and putrefaction, which in each case depend very heavily on the storage conditions and climatic circumstances, such as temperature and humidity. Putrefaction is caused by bacteria that partly already exist on the skin, in the oral cavity, in the nose and throat region and in the intestines. They can also partly derive from the surrounding milieu.

In the process much gas is created which, as a rule, goes hand-in-hand with an alteration in the colour of organs and tissues and might lead to a liquefaction of soft tissue and skeletisation of the corpse. Essentially taking place without oxygen, this is contrasted by decomposition, a dry, acidic process taking place in the presence of oxygen. Besides bacteria, mould fungi in particular can participate in the decomposition of tissue too. In addition, fly maggots especially can promote a quick degradation of a dead body.

The different processes vary considerably according to burial method of the deceased or storage of a corpse. Nevertheless, in most cases a complete degradation of the soft tissue and internal organs, and thus a skeletisation of a body, takes place sooner or later. Bones often survive in graves for many centuries, or even millennia, due to

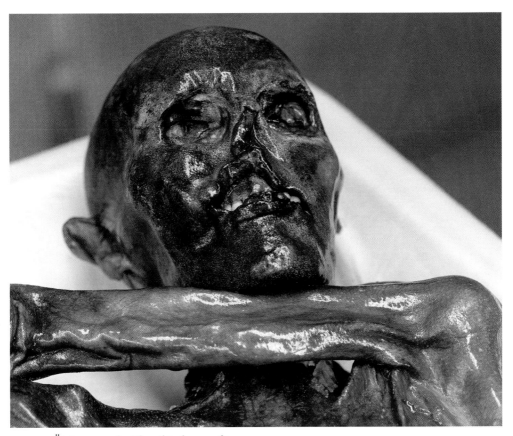

Ötzi, covered with a thin layer of ice.

their high mineral content, although especially in moist or acidic soils a complete disintegration of the skeleton can occur too.

Therefore, very specific conditions must be given for the mummification of a corpse, which stop the natural process of putrefaction that starts immediately after death under normal circumstances. It is important that these conditions are maintained as otherwise the processes decomposing the body can resume again at a later date. An important prerequisite is that water drains from the dead body as soon as possible. This can ensue by means of a dry environment and can be supported by good ventilation.

With the rapid dehydration of the body, the microbial activities that occur in the context of putrefaction are impeded and might cease entirely. This causes a leathery solidification of the skin and a fixation of the posture taken up at the occurrence of death. Typical examples for dry mummification are, firstly, the numerous mummies in churches and crypts, which were most often preserved by a combination of low humidity and sufficient ventilation. Further examples are represented by mummies from various desert regions, such as the Libyan Desert or the Atacama Desert in northern Chile. Here the burial of the dead in the hot, dry desert sand led to a rapid dehydration and thus to a mummification of the corpses. The earliest Egyptian mummies came about in this natural manner through burial in the desert sand.

Another form of mummification is the freezing of the body after death. With appropriate climatic preconditions, as they prevail, for example, in the polar and sub-polar regions of the earth or at high altitudes, glaciers and in permafrost soils, preservation of corpses can also occur. Particularly impressive are the members of the Franklin expedition, who are buried in the cemetery of the Beechey Islands in the Canadian Arctic.

During the expedition of the British officer and polar explorer Sir John Franklin from 1845 to 1848, all 129 participants died tragically in an attempt to sail the Northwest Passage from east to west for the first time. When opening three of the graves, the almost perfectly mummified bodies of three expedition members were found, who were surrounded by ice and had survived more than 150 years due to burial in permafrost.

A further example for the preservation in a cold climate is represented by the mummies from the settlement of Qilakitsoq in western Greenland. In two graves eight mummies were found here, which came about in a natural manner through a combination of low temperatures and dry air, i.e. a kind of freeze-drying process. The deceased, whose death was dated 1475 AD and who are among the direct ancestors of the Inuit living in the eastern Arctic, were fully dressed and replete with furs, jackets and trousers. Another prominent example for preservation in ice is the glacial mummy Ötzi. In this case too the predominantly low temperatures, and a regular covering of ice and snow, presumably combined with strong sunlight and winds, led to a preservation of the man within the ice for several thousand years.

Bog body of the Tollund Man.

Mummification can occur if a burial is carried out under almost complete exclusion of air or if the deceased is laid to rest in a highly oxygen-deficient environment. So it is assumed in the case of some mummies from the Asian region, for example in China and South Korea, that the interment in several nested wooden coffins and the sealing of the graves with limestone or large amounts of charcoal and sediment has led to a largely oxygen-free atmosphere inside the coffin and thus has facilitated the mummification process.

The prime example for mummification in oxygen-deficient milieu, however, are the bog bodies. These are found almost exclusively in moorlands of Northwest Europe, especially around the North Sea, i.e. Denmark, Northern Germany, the Netherlands, Great Britain and Ireland. In principle the oxygen-deficient surroundings and the presence of tanning substances and humic acids bring about a preservation of corpses in the bog. Yet we have to distinguish between hill moor and low moor, which have a different chemical composition leading to different manners of preservation of the bodies.

In the hill moor a very acidic milieu prevails, which attacks both bones and objects made of horn and iron and can dissolve them. Tanning substances and humic acids are present here too, which may cause a tanning of the skin and a red staining of the hair. In contrast, the low moor has a rather alkaline environment, which is conducive to bone preservation, but has an adverse effect on skin and other soft tissue. Therefore, the state of preservation can vary considerably with bog bodies. The classic representative of this type and probably the most famous bog body is Tollund Man, who was found in Denmark and originates from the third century AD. The astonishingly well-preserved face of the approximately 40-year-old man, in which we can still discern wrinkles and beard stubble, gives him a special personal expression. He lies on his side in a relaxed posture, although a rope around the neck hints that he fell victim to a violent death by hanging or strangulation.

The Lindow Man, found in England, became the subject of extensive scientific studies too. He died in an equally unnatural manner. His skull and the cervical spine showed massive signs of blows that were inflicted on him from behind. It is disputed if in addition he was strangled and received a stab in the throat.

Among numerous bog bodies, further executed or murdered persons are found, for example the Grauballe Man found in Denmark or the man from Neu Versen (Lower Saxony) called Red Francis due to his reddish brown stained hair. Both were killed by having their throat cut and subsequently buried on the moor. Bog bodies without any sign of violence are found too, for which merely the place of burial has to be considered unusual.

The manners of mummification described so far all took place without the influence of man or the purport to preserve the deceased in any form. Nobody reckoned in the cases of the sailors buried in permafrost or of the bog bodies that they would be rediscovered many years later as mummies. Here we speak of natural or spontaneous mummification, one of the three main forms of mummification.

Artificial mummification stands in contrast to this. Here the deceased deliberately undergo a treatment with the expressed aim to preserve their body for an afterlife. The underlying mechanisms are absolutely identical, since here too it was attempted to stop the natural processes of putrefaction and to halt them in perpetuity. For this reason the ancient Egyptians used large amounts of natron for their rituals of mummification, as this accelerated the dehydration of the body and protected it from decomposition. Additional measures, like the use of resins, oils and bitumen, the removal of the

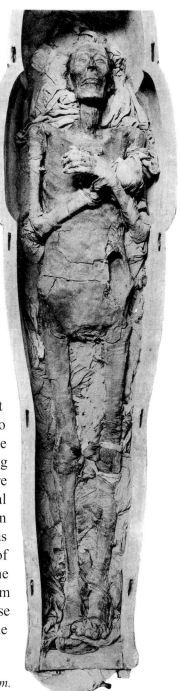

Mummy of Ramses II, Cairo Museum.

17

Two embalmed mummies in the Capuchin crypt, Palermo.

internal organs and the brain, and the wrapping of the dried corpse in numerous linen bandages, helped to preserve the body permanently. Artificial mummification also existed in some South American cultures, for example with the Chinchorro, who elaborately prepared and preserved their dead long before the Egyptians.

Modern forms of artificial mummification are the methods of Southern Italian embalmers, who preserved bodies with the aid of liquids containing heavy metals at first, and later used embalming fluids based on formalin. The latter method is still in use today, embalming the deceased for lying in state, or body donors for the training of medical students in anatomy. Yet it is not based on the principle that the body is dehydrated quickly, but the disintegration of the corpse is prevented by the injection of putrefaction-resistant substances, at first highly toxic arsenic or mercury compounds, and later formalin solutions or carbolic acid.

The third form of mummification is an intermediate form of the two mentioned so far. The natural-intentional mummification is based on the natural processes described above, which bring about a preservation of the body, but these were used deliberately because of cultural or religious reasons, or even enhanced. Examples of this are the highland mummies of South America, which were buried or sacrificed in the high altitudes of the Andes, as it was intuitively known that the climatic conditions there led to dehydration and preservation of the body.

Female child mummy, Llullaillaco, Northern Chile.

Many church mummies are due to the clerics' knowledge of the preserving effect of an interment in a crypt. Especially on Sicily specific rooms or areas are found in numerous churches, as for example the Colatoi in the Capuchin crypt in Palermo, in which the deceased were laid to rest specifically in order to inter them in crypts or catacombs after mummification has ensued. However, as a rule the bodies were treated merely superficially, for example by washing with vinegar or application of aromas or herbs. A preparation in the sense of an opening of the body cavity, removal of organs or filling with embalming substances did not take place in this case and therefore we count these forms as natural-intentional mummification.

2

Where in the world do mummies exist?

The geographic distribution of mummies

Mummies are not limited to a few cultures and geographic regions but are found in almost all areas around the globe. The map gives an overview of the most important mummies and their dates. The mummies introduced in more detail here are marked accordingly. While looking at the map, it becomes clear that mummies extend very far back in history and are found on all continents. Naturally a certain clustering of finds is shown in regions where a natural mummification process is promoted by climatic conditions. This is the case with the dry desert regions in America, Africa and Asia, with the cold areas of the polar and sub-polar region, with the highlands in South America, and with the moorlands in northern Europe. Mummies are found in higher numbers there, where due to cultural or religious influences, artificial or natural-intentional mummification was practised. This applies especially to pharaonic Egypt but also to the church mummies of Southern Italy and to many Asian mummies, for example the mummified monks in Japan, Thailand and Vietnam, and the Scythian ice mummies of Siberia.

North America
1. Mummies of the Franklin expedition: three sailors buried in permafrost and ice, Beechey Islands, Canada, 1846.

2. Family of Utqiagvik: victims of a collapsed wooden hut with two surviving female ice mummies, Alaska, USA, c. 1500 AD.
3. Kwäday Dän Ts'inchi (person found from distant past) or Canadian Iceman: natural mummy of a man, British Columbia, Canada, 1670 – 1850 AD.
4. Mummies of the Aleutians: embalmed bodies in rock shelters and caves, Aleutian Islands, Alaska, USA, c. 1700 – 1800 AD.
5. Spirit Cave Man: natural mummy of a man, Spirit Cave grotto, Nevada, USA, 7415 BC.
6. Mummies of the Hisatsinom (Anasazi): c. one hundred mummies preserved by dehydration, in some cases indications of organ removal, Four Corners, South-West USA, 100 – 1200 AD.
7. Lost John: cave visitor killed in an accident, Mammoth Cave, Kentucky, USA, 200 BC.
8. John Paul Jones: corpse of the American captain and freedom fighter mummified in alcohol, Annapolis, Maryland, USA, 1792 AD.
9. Elmer McCurdy: body of an outlaw mummified by an arsenic solution, Oklahoma, USA, 1911 AD.

Central America
10. Mummies of Guanajuato: more than 100 natural mummies in the town cemetery, Museo de las Momias, Guanajuato, Mexico, c. 1800 AD.
11. Mummies of Chihuahua: two naturally preserved mummies from a cave near Chihuahua, Mexico, 690 – 610 BC.

South America
12. Mummies of Musica: mummies of highland inhabitants, both naturally derived and artificially preserved, Central Columbia, 1000 – 1520 AD.
13. Mummies of the Jivaro: mummified shrunken heads, eastern Ecuador, c. 1600 – 1980 AD.
14. Mummies of Paracas: interments tied into textile bundles; Paracas peninsula, Peru, c. 600 BC – 200 AD.
15. Mummies of the Nazca culture: spontaneously mummified mummy bundles, and trophy heads, Nazca, Peru, c. 250 BC – 750 AD.

16. Mummies of the Chachapoya: artificial mummies of the 'cloud people', Lake Condor, Andes, northern Peru, 800 – 1400 AD.
17. Mummies of the Moche culture: natural mummies with body paintings, among them Lady Cao, north-western Peru, c. 100 – 800 AD.
18. Mummies of the Huari and Tiahuanaco: mummy bundles, partly decorated with false heads, coastal region of Peru and Andes highlands in Peru, Bolivia and Chile, c. 600 – 900 AD.
19. Mummies of the Inca: spontaneous and natural-intentional mummy bundles and human sacrifices, among them Juanita (Ice Maiden), occasionally indications of artificial mummification, Arequipa and further sites in Peru, c. 1400 –1500 AD.
20. Mummies of the Chinchorro: one hundred to two hundred artificially preserved mummies, Arica, Chile, c. 7000 – 1500 BC.
21. Mummies of Llullaillaco: three mummified human sacrifices found at an altitude of 6,700m, Llullaillaco Mountain, Salta, Argentina, c. 1400 AD.
22. Evita Perón: embalmed corpse of the revered wife of the Argentinian president, Buenos Aires, Argentina, 1952 AD.

Europe
23. Mummies of Qilakitsoq: six women and two children, fully dressed, Nuussuaq peninsula, Greenland, Denmark, c. 1475 AD.
24. Bog bodies from North Europe: Tollund Man, Lindow Man, man from Neu Versen (Red Francis) and numerous naturally preserved finds in moors, Denmark, Northern Germany, England, Ireland, and the Netherlands, c. 800 BC – 1400 AD (skeletal finds as early as 8000 BC).
25. Mummies of Vác: naturally mummified corpses that were found in a crypt, Vác, Hungary, 1731 – c. 1800 AD.
26. Sicilian church mummies: mummies of clerics and citizens, among them Rosalia Lombardo (Capuchin crypt, Palermo), natural, natural-intentional and artificial mummies, Sicily, Italy, 1599 – 1920 AD.
27. Church and crypt mummies: natural and natural-intentional mummies in many parts of Europe – Italy, Germany, Norway, Austria, Spain, Poland, Czech Republic, etc, c. thirteenth to twentieth centuries AD.

28. Guancha mummies: artificially preserved cave burials, Canary Islands, Spain, 400 – 1500 AD.
29. Ötzi, the man from the ice: glacial mummy from the Ötztal Alps, Similaun, South Tirol, Italy, c. 5300 BC.
30. Lenin: embalmed corpse of the state founder of the Soviet Union, Moscow, Russia, 1924 AD.

Africa
31. Egyptian mummies: natural mummies from the predynastic period and artificial mummies from pharaonic times, among them Tutankhamen, Ramses II, Akhenaten and Seti I, Egypt, c. 4000 BC – 400 AD.
32. Mummy from the Libyan Desert: child mummy naturally preserved by dehydration, Central Libya, 3455 BC.
33. Kouga mummy: single mummy find in South Africa, wildlife reserve Baviaanskloof, South Africa, c. 50 BC.

Asia
34. Jordanian mummies: partly and wholly naturally mummified corpses in a cemetery, Khirbet Qazone, Jordan, 0 – 200 AD.
35. Iranian salt mummies: five victims accidentally buried in a salt mine, Khehrabad, Zanyan province, Iran, 600 – 400 BC and 400 – 600 AD.
36. Mummies of the Scythes: artificially preserved corpses of the Pazyryk culture, among them the Ice Princess (Altaic Lady), Altai mountain range, Siberia, Russia, c. 500 – 300 BC.
37. Mummies of the Tarim Basin: natural mummies from the Central Asian Tarim Basin situated along the Silk Route, Käwirgul, Yanbulag and other sites, West China, 1800 BC – 1000 AD.
38. Mummies of the Han Dynasty: humidly preserved corpses of the Chinese Han period (206 BC – 220 AD), among them Lady Dai, Changsha, Hunan Province, China.
39. Fujiwara mummies: mummified bodies of the Japanese ruling family, Chuson-ji Temple, Hiraizumi, Japan, c. 1100 AD.
40. Buddhist monks: self-mummification of Buddhist monks in Japan, Thailand and Vietnam, c. 1300 – 1903 AD.

41. Mummies of the Ibaloi: mummies dried by smoke and fire, Kabayan, Benquet province, Philippines, c. 1500 – 1800 AD.
42. Mao Zedong: founder of the People's Republic of China, Beijing, China, 1976 AD.
43. Ho Chi Min: founder of modern Vietnam, Hanoi, Vietnam, 1969 AD.

Oceania and Australia

44. Mummies of Koke: dried and cured mummies of the Anga tribe that were placed in rock shelters, Koke, Papua New Guinea, 1800 – 1950 AD.
45. Mummies of the Torres Straight: nine artificial mummies that were painted with red ochre and decorated with shells, Torres Straight, North Australia, before and around 1900 AD.
46. Australian mummies: artificial mummification by evisceration and dehydration, Queensland, Australia, before and around 1900 AD.
47. Maori mummies: prepared and tattooed heads of leaders or high ranking tribe members, New Zealand, c. 1600 – 1800 AD.
48. Mummies of the Cook Islands, Tahiti and Samoa: mummies prepared by drying and incisions, Pacific Islands, before and around 1900 AD.

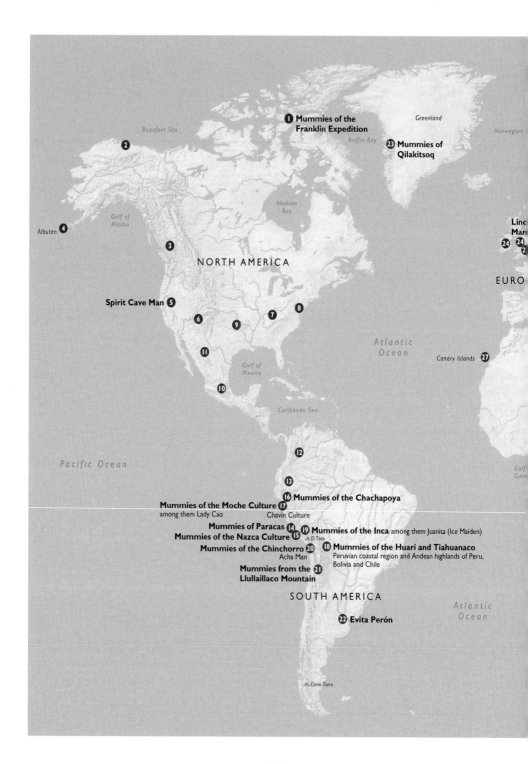

① Mummies of the
Franklin Expedition

Greenland

Norwegian

Beaufort Sea

Baffin Bay

②

㉓ Mummies of
Qilakitsoq

*Gulf of
Alaska*

*Hudson
Bay*

Aleüten **④**

Linc
Man

③

㉔ **㉔**
②

NORTH AMERICA

EURO

Spirit Cave Man **⑤**

⑥ **⑦** **⑧**

⑨

*Atlantic
Ocean*

Canary Islands **㉗**

⑪

*Gulf of
Mexico*

⑩

Pacific Ocean

Caribbean Sea

⑫

*Gulf
Guin*

⑬

⑯ Mummies of the Chachapoya

Mummies of the Moche Culture **⑰**
among them Lady Cao

Chavin Culture

Mummies of Paracas **⑭** **⑲** Mummies of the Inca among them Juanita (Ice Maiden)
Mummies of the Nazca Culture **⑮** ▲ *El Toro*

Mummies of the Chinchorro **⑳** **⑱** Mummies of the Huari and Tiahuanaco
Acha Man Peruvian coastal region and Andean highlands of Peru,
Bolivia and Chile

Mummies from the **㉑**
Llullaillaco Mountain

SOUTH AMERICA

*Atlantic
Ocean*

㉒ Evita Perón

▲ *Cerro Torre*

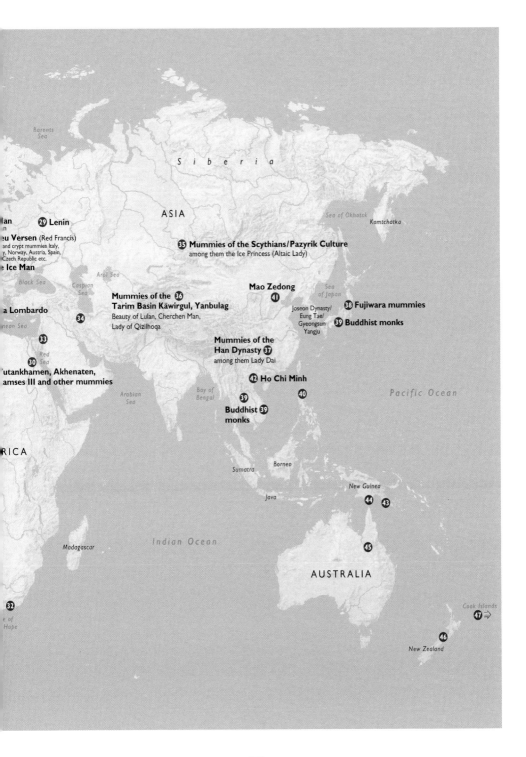

Barents
Sea

Siberia

ASIA

Sea of Okhotsk
Kamtchatka

lan
n **29** **Lenin**

eu Versen (Red Francis)
and crypt mummies Italy,
y, Norway, Austria, Spain,
Czech Republic etc.
e Ice Man

Aral Sea

35 **Mummies of the Scythians/Pazyrik Culture**
among them the Ice Princess (Altaic Lady)

Black Sea

Caspian
Sea

Mummies of the 36
a Lombardo
34
Tarim Basin Käwirgul, Yanbulag
Beauty of Lulan, Cherchen Man,
Lady of Qizilhoqa

Mao Zedong
41

Sea
of Japan

Joseon Dynasty/
Eung Tae/
Gyeongsun
Yangju

38 **Fujiwara mummies**
39 **Buddhist monks**

nean Sea

33

Red
Sea

30

Mummies of the
Han Dynasty 37
among them Lady Dai

utankhamen, Akhenaten,
amses III and other mummies

Arabian
Sea

Bay of
Bengal

42 **Ho Chi Minh**

39

40

Pacific Ocean

Buddhist 39
monks

RICA

Borneo

Sumatra

Java

New Guinea

44 **43**

Madagascar

Indian Ocean

45

AUSTRALIA

32

e of
Hope

Cook Islands
47 ⇒

46

New Zealand

27

3

How do mummies date?

The age of mummies

Again and again reports of finding the oldest mummy in the world appear in the media. Most often no distinction is made whether it is a natural or an artificial mummy, and under which circumstances the mummification and the enduring preservation of the find came about. The following are, therefore, the earliest securely dated mummies known so far and will give an impression of the time in which human bodies were preserved, and of how far natural-intentional and artificial mummification date back.

The artificial preservation of human remains is, of course, primarily known from ancient Egypt in the age of such great rulers as Tutankhamen and Ramses. Indeed, in the Egyptian New Kingdom age, c. 1550 – 1080 BC, mummification reached its peak, during which the technique and the efficiency of the procedure attained their fullest development. However, the beginnings of embalming date back to the Old Kingdom, i.e. to approximately 2500 BC.

A few years ago the mummified remains of an official of the Egyptian 1st Dynasty (5,000 years ago) were found, which bore indications of the application of a resin-like substance. Therefore, this find counts among the earliest records of artificial mummification in ancient Egypt. Before this, even much earlier mummies of the Egyptian predynastic period (c. 4000 – 3000 BC) are found. A well-known example is the mummy with the nickname Ginger, which is exhibited in the British Museum, London, and dates to c. 3400 BC. This is the very well-preserved mummy of a man that was excavated in a tomb in the desert near the site of Gebelein together with five other mummies. Since 2004 the nickname is no longer officially used due to ethical considerations on the part of the museum. The mummy is an early example of natural mummification, the extraordinarily good state of preservation of which is due to the dry bedding in the desert sand. It can be compared to the glacial mummy Ötzi, which was dated to 3300 BC, and is equally an example for natural mummification. In the case of the man from the ice, this is due to his permanent resting place in snow and ice. Additional finds from Libya point to the fact that there too the dead were already artificially mummified 5,500 years ago. Consequently, to our current knowledge, mummies of the Old World date back to approximately 3500 BC.

In contrast, considerably earlier mummies are found on the American continent. South America offers an immense wealth of mummies, which are far less-known than the Egyptian mummies but are equally intriguing and of great scientific interest. In the dry desert regions of Peru and Chile in particular, but also in the Andes highlands, ideal climatic preconditions exist to enable natural preservation of dead human bodies. The mummies were predominantly in the western part of South America and range from Columbia via Ecuador to Argentina. Among them are some of the earliest mummies of the world known so far.

In the Atacama Desert, one of the driest regions of the globe, the Chinchorro people lived since the seventh millennium BC. From this culture the first artificial mummies originate. At first the Chinchorro only preserved their deceased children, then later all ages. The earliest finds were dated to 5050 BC and are more than 1,000 years older than the earliest Egyptian mummies. In addition, early examples of natural mummies are found, among them one of the earliest attested mummies of the world, the so-called Acha Man. He was found in the proximity of Antofagasta Harbour and has been dated to c. 7000 BC. Furthermore, occasional finds from other South American regions have become known, which are likewise estimated to be very old.

For example, in 1964 mountaineers discovered a mummy, probably 7,000 years old, on the Andean peak Cerro Torre near the border between Argentina and Chile (San Juan province). In Peru, mummies exist that are even estimated at an age of up to 10,000 years. However, in these cases thorough examinations on the exact date and cultural background are still missing. As long as these are not available, we have to regard the Chinchorro mummies as the earliest mummies of South America known so far.

The mummy of a man between 45 to 55 years of age, which was found in the Spirit Cave Grotto in Nevada (USA), is more than 400 years older again than the first Chinchorro mummies. These human remains are a partially skeletal and dehydrated corpse on which skull and shoulders still bore skin and hair. In 1994 the mummy, which was initially considered to be much younger, was examined by radiocarbon dating, resulting in the astonishing age of 9,415 +/- twenty-five years. Therefore the Spirit Cave Man is currently viewed as the earliest mummy of the world.

Mummification is by no means only a phenomenon of past ages and cultures it still exists today. In Europe naturally preserved mummies are found in numerous churches and crypts, laid to rest there well into the nineteenth century, and which were mummified primarily due to the favourable climatic conditions. In addition, at the beginning of the nineteenth century the technique of embalming became prevalent in Europe. An arsenic liquid was injected into the body of the deceased for its preservation by way of the large blood vessels, such as the jugular or the femoral arteries. This method, which made the opening of the body superfluous, was further refined in southern Italy and an attempt was increasingly made to find alternatives to the use of the toxic heavy metals arsenic and mercury. The Sicilian taxidermist and embalmer Alfredo Salafia was one of the first to succeed in this. He developed his own embalming fluid based on formalin (formaldehyde solution in water), glycerine and alcohol. This made the use of toxic heavy metals unnecessary, and Salafia was able to achieve impressive results with his new method. Some examples of his embalming skills are still visible today in the Capuchin crypt in Palermo, among which is the impressively well-preserved Rosalia Lombardo, who died in 1920 at the tender age of 2.

The use of formalin gained general acceptance in the medical preparation of human tissue (anatomy). It is still used today in the USA for the embalming of corpses in order to enable a lying in state. The technique of embalming was used in particular for prominent personalities such as popes, members of ruling families and politicians. The best-known examples for this are Lenin, Mao Zedong and Evita Perón.

On the whole, it is no longer customary today – due to religious, ethical and socio-cultural reasons – to prepare the dead with the aim of a permanent preservation of the bodily shell for eternity. In general, these days embalming serves the temporary retention of the body for lying in state or the training of medical students in anatomy. Exceptions are perhaps the plastinates of the dissector Gunther von Hagens, and the attempt of often seriously ill people to survive by means of so-called cryopreservation in tanks of liquid nitrogen in order to be reanimated and cured in the far future, when medical procedures will have advanced accordingly.

4

What do mummies tell us?

The scientific study of mummies

The interest in mummies in Europe dates back to the thirteenth to sixteenth centuries. At that time the drug mumia, consisting of pulverised Egyptian mummies, was in great demand and enjoyed widespread use. In the scientific sphere the British surgeon and antiquary Thomas Joseph Pettigrew was the first to present a detailed study on an Egyptian mummy. In his book published in 1834, *A History of Egyptian Mummies*, he described in detail the unwrapping of a mummy and discussed the history and technique of mummification in ancient Egypt.

Recently the study of mummified finds has developed into a serious scientific branch, in which a wide range of modern procedures from the areas of medicine, molecular biology, chemistry and physics find their application. The different examination methods are now used to reconstruct the historical life circumstances, dietary habits, diseases, origin and genetic relationships of human kind on the basis of mummies all over the world. In several molecular studies, for example, different infectious diseases could be attested, which have allowed deep insights into the occurrence, the spread and the evolution of diseases such as tuberculosis, malaria or leishmaniasis.

The good state of soft tissues in mummies has enabled the conduct of broad studies on the occurrence of cancers and vascular diseases, for example arteriosclerosis. In recent years, even methods of modern nanotechnology have been applied, which provided important findings regarding the preservation of proteins, for example collagen, and red blood cells in mummies, and which allowed new insights into the mummification processes of natural mummies.

Medical imaging procedures play an important role in mummy studies, such as radiology, computed tomography and magnetic resonance tomography, which all permit non-destructive examinations.

In principle, invasive and non-invasive procedures are distinguished within the examination methods. The non-invasive or non-destructive methods make it unnecessary to take tissue samples from the mummy. The mummy can be kept in its original state. This is an aspect gaining increasing importance as mummies have to be considered as cultural heritage, too, which may not simply be sampled and damaged or even destroyed. Furthermore, the question of an ethically appropriate approach to mummies is of importance, since they are first and foremost deceased persons who have to be treated with dignity and respect. For example, mummy autopsies are now a thing of the past, since these led, by-and-large, to a destruction of the mummy. Besides, thanks to the advancement of the medical-scientific examination methods, the same insights can be gained without destruction, or at least with little sample material.

Radiological and endoscopic examinations
Radiology probably constitutes the most important non-invasive examination technique within mummy studies. With the aid of X-ray, computed tomography and magnetic resonance tomography insights into the insides of mummies can be gained, and due to the steadily improving resolution the tiniest details can be worked out. Classical X-ray played a great role, especially at the beginning of the scientific examination of mummies. It was already successfully applied to two mummies of the Senckenberg Museum of Natural History one year after the discovery of the Roentgen rays. Furthermore, the Egyptian royal mummies in the Cairo Museum were X-rayed in the sixties and seventies.

Through the development of computer tomograph and the advancements in computer-based image post-processing, which have led to a significant improvement of the radiological diagnostic, conventional X-ray was more and more pushed back. For the first time it became possible to produce not only survey radiographs (summation

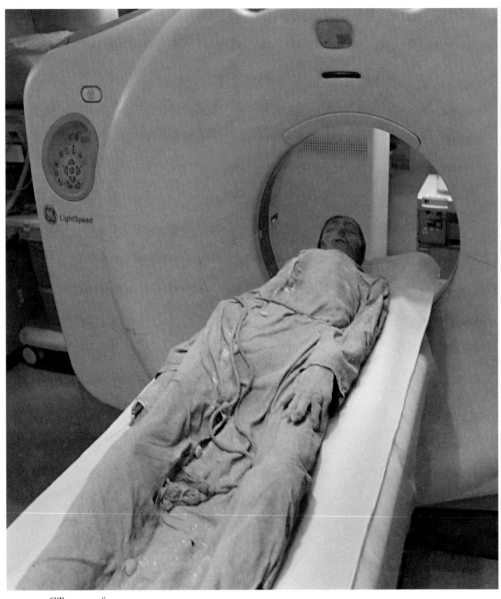

CT scan of a mummy.

images), but even virtual three-dimensional reconstructions of internal structures, for example the skull. Analog to the medical-radiological diagnostic treatment of mummies too, fine structures and their alterations can also be attested far better with the computer tomograph.

Complicated fractures, but also vessels, passages of vessels, calcifications, etc, can be captured much more clearly and in detail. In addition, an exact localisation of artefacts, such as amulets or mummification materials, is possible. Yet for a first glimpse into the interior of a mummy and to capture simple fractures, for example, conventional X-ray represents a sensible alternative.

It is not always possible to transport mummies for an examination to a hospital with a CT device. For an examination of mummies in situ, i.e. the find spot, portable X-ray machines are often suitable, since these can be easily transported and are simple in their use. Mobile CT devices represent another possibility. These are mounted on a truck and can be brought to the mummies. For example, the Egyptian royal mummies in Cairo and some mummies from the Capuchin crypt in Palermo were examined in this manner.

Magnetic resonance tomography (nuclear spin tomography) was classified as unusable on mummies for a long time, since this examination method is based on the stimulus of hydrogen nuclei (water content of organs), and usually little or no water is present in mummies. However, through the development of new software, images of mummy tissue have now been successfully generated and certain structures, for example intervertebral discs, have been visualised in particular detail.

The different radiological procedures, and especially computed tomography, in this way offer the opportunity to scientists to determine the age and sex of mummies in a destruction-free manner, to find out details of the mummification method, to identify amulets and embalming material (bandages, bitumen, Nile mud, etc), to diagnose diseases (tumours, fractures, arteriosclerosis, injuries and organ alterations and disorders), and occasionally even to receive clues of the cause of death, as we will see in the chapters on Ötzi and Ramses III.

Another non-invasive examination method is endoscopy, provided that access points such as natural or post-mortem body orifices – occurring after death or in the course of mummification – exist. The use of endoscopes offers the opportunity to receive insights into (almost) enclosed cavities of bodies. With this a second method for an examination free of or at least minimal in destruction is available besides X-ray and CT analysis, which additionally offers the opportunity to make small samples of untouched biological material accessible via working channels of a few millimetres. A specific application of endoscopic investigations lies in the sphere of otolaryngology, as with the aid of endoscopic procedures the cavities within the skull can be examined. Today an application on mummies under excavation conditions is perfectly possible.

Biochemical and histological procedures
The analysis of proteins in mummy tissue gives information on the state of preservation of tissue and some indications on specific metabolic conditions, for example chronic malnutrition. The main target of early biochemical analyses was, as a rule, collagen in its different forms. This primary supportive protein of the body is responsible for the elasticity of skin and the internal organs, but is also an important component of bones, cartilage and tendons. It is characterised by a considerable resilience against diagenesis and autolysis and is often still well-preserved in many mummies. The results of an analysis of amino acids can provide clues to the state of preservation of bone collagen and a potential addition of foreign proteins, for example external contaminations. Further biochemical analyses, for example of specific cell proteins or enzymes, were occasionally successful for mummy tissue but have so far only provided limited additional information.

Histological examinations are a widespread diagnostic method in medical daily routine today, which also possess considerable importance for mummy studies. It is crucial for a successful histological analysis to rehydrate the dried material, which was also chemically treated during the embalming. In several studies on mummy tissue it was shown that the application of a mixture of formalin and detergents, potentially with an addition of alcoholic solutions, can deliver satisfactory histomorphological results. Besides survey staining, for example haematoxylin-eosin, and special staining, for example van Gieson, PAS, occasionally immunohistochemical procedures have been applied successfully so far.

For bone samples a decalcification is also necessary ahead of the embedding in paraffin, before routine staining can be applied. With the aid of histology different types of tissue or internal organs can still be identified in many cases. This can be of great importance if the soft tissue can no longer be clearly addressed due to severe dehydration or if internal organs were removed and placed into vessels, for example. The examination of tissue-thin sections under the microscope can provide clues to different diseases and injuries. For instance, eggs of parasites can be detected in the intestines or other organs.

Molecular biological analyses

A tremendous extension of the diagnostic spectrum for mummy studies took place in recent years with the use of molecular biological methods. Through the development of the polymerase chain reaction (PCR) it has become possible to determine ancient DNA (aDNA) in mummy and skeletal material. With the aid of the extraction of aDNA from tissue samples and subsequent targeted amplification of characteristic sections of the genome pathogenic germs, could be detected. In addition, human genome sections of the individuals examined can be analysed for molecular determination of sex, clarification of familial relationships and the detection of inherent malformations, which are caused in the human genome by mutation. Yet limits are set to the aDNA technology, which are primarily founded in the rapid degradation of DNA after the death of an individual and in the danger of carry-over and contamination by modern DNA.

Recently, the development of new sequencing technologies, 'next generation sequencing' or 'whole genome sequencing', has opened up entirely new possibilities for the molecular biological examination of mummies. It has become possible to reconstruct the entire genetic make-up of a mummy, or even skeleton, on the basis of little sample material. Extensive information on genetic origin, appearance, for example the colour of eyes and hair, body functions, blood type, lactose intolerance, and occurrence of diseases and genetically determined medical conditions can be studied. The results of such an examination will be shown using the example of the man from the ice further below.

5

Mummies from different regions of the world

In this section the most important mummies from the different regions of the world are introduced. After a general introduction, some particular representatives of the respective cultures and dates will be described in detail, especially going into the latest scientific results.

Mummies from South America

Mummies and mummification play an important role in pre-Columbian cultures of South America. On no other continent is such a variety of different mummies and forms of mummification spanning many thousand years found. In principle, mummies are found in almost all South American countries, but are present predominantly in the western regions along the Pacific coast and the highlands of the Andes. Circumstances that have influenced the natural as well as the natural-intentional and artificial mummification are probably the specific climatic conditions in this region. On the one hand, extremely arid desert is situated along the coast to the west of the continent, for example the Atamaca and Sechura Deserts. On the other hand, equally favourable climatic conditions exist in the western Andes. On the almost 7,000m-high mountain chain temperatures are very low during the night, and during the day very strong sunlight prevails. To this is added a low oxygen content in high altitudes that further promotes a natural preservation of biological materials. Numerous valleys with rivers and brooks have formed within the mountain chains, which also offered good conditions for the development of advanced civilisations.

Female mummy with two children, Quiani region, Northern Chile.

In South America the entire spectrum of mummification is found, from naturally preserved mummies to artificial mummies that have been preserved by organ removal, external treatment with embalming substances or similar, as well as natural-intentional mummies, where for example the corpses were buried in high altitudes or were tied into bundles and deliberately subjected to a natural process of mummification.

The earliest mummies known so far from South America have to be of the Chinchorro culture, the earliest records of which date back 9,000 years. Since at least 5050 BC, the Chinchorro practised a very specific method of mummification with an elaborate preparation of dead bodies including organ removal. This will be discussed in detail in the chapter on Chinchorro mummies.

On the Paracas peninsula in the south of Peru, the mummified remains of the Paracas culture are found, which lasted from 600 BC to 200 AD. In the earlier phase of the culture the deceased persons were predominantly interred in shaft tombs or cavernas. The mummies found therein are primarily older female individuals showing wedge-shaped deformations of the skull. Furthermore, trepanations, i.e. openings of the skull, were found in high numbers, which were carried out during the individual's life and which were survived by the affected people in most cases. The dead were tied up in a crouched position and furnished with abundant grave goods such as food, amulets, etc.

In the later phase of the Paracas culture entire necropoleis with numerous subterranean tombs were constructed. Here 429 mummy bundles in total were found, predominantly adult men. The question of how far this is a natural mummification process or whether this was artificially promoted has not be clarified. We can assume with certainty that no organ removal took place. Yet occasionally clues for dehydration by fire or smoke could be attested on the mummies.

Subsequent to the Paracas culture the advanced civilisation of the Nazca developed in the region of the city with the same name, lasting from 200 BC to 600 AD. The culture became particularly renowned through the gigantic drawings of symbols and animals (geoglyphs) located on the high plain between the Pacific Ocean and the Andes, generally called Nazca lines.

Chachapoya mummy from Leymebamba.

Male child mummy, Llullaillaco, Northern Chile.

In the Nazca culture, the dead were likewise interred as mummy bundles in the extremely arid desert region of Atamaca and in the Palpa valley. Here too the artificial deformation of skulls was practised. In addition so-called trophy skulls were found, i.e. specifically mummified heads that were mostly attached to strings and carried around. These have been generally viewed as war booty, but more recent studies show that the dead were relatives or at least inhabitants of the same village. It is simply unclear if these are human sacrifices or a special cult of the dead.

A different type of mummification is attested by the mummies of the Chavin and the Moche cultures at the northern coast of Peru. Here the deceased persons were interred in outstretched positions, and apparently no artificial mummification took place. In the Moche culture examples of body painting on mummies are found, for example an arm tattooed with animal symbols, and also the tomb of a female leader or warrior, Lady Cao (c. 400 BC), equipped with numerous weapons.

With the beginning of the period called the middle horizon around 600 AD, the Tiahuanaco and Huari cultures emerged in the highlands, which grew into empires. Here too crouched inhumation was carried out, and sometimes the mummy bundles were decorated with dummy heads. The culture of the Chachapoya existed from approximately 800 to 1400 AD, the name of which means cloud people or mist warriors, which they received from the Inca. In the 1990s a large burial site of the Chachapoya was discovered in the north of Peru near Lake Condor in the Andes. The dead were mummified by organ removal and drainage of bodily fluids and buried with grave goods in caves and rock shelters.

Numerous further mummies exist from the time of the Inca, who built up a large empire from 1438 to 1533 AD stretching from the Columbian border into Chile. The royal mummies of the Inca capital, Cuzco, were especially venerated and presented during the ritual of the sun festival. Unfortunately these mummies did not survive as they were destroyed by the Spanish conquerors.

There are numerous indications from the Inca period for the execution of ritual human sacrifices. In this connection, children predominantly were interred in the high altitudes of the Andes. Examples for this are the child mummies that were discovered on the Llullaillac mountain at a height of 6,700m on the border between Argentina and Chile, the mummy Juanita from the top of the volcano Ampato, a mummy on the Picchu Picchu mountain at a height of 5,670m, and the mummy of a young man on the El Toro mountain.

With the conquest of South America by the Spanish and the beginning of the colonial era the tradition of mummification ended. Therefore there are hardly any mummies from the period between 1534 and 1821 AD.

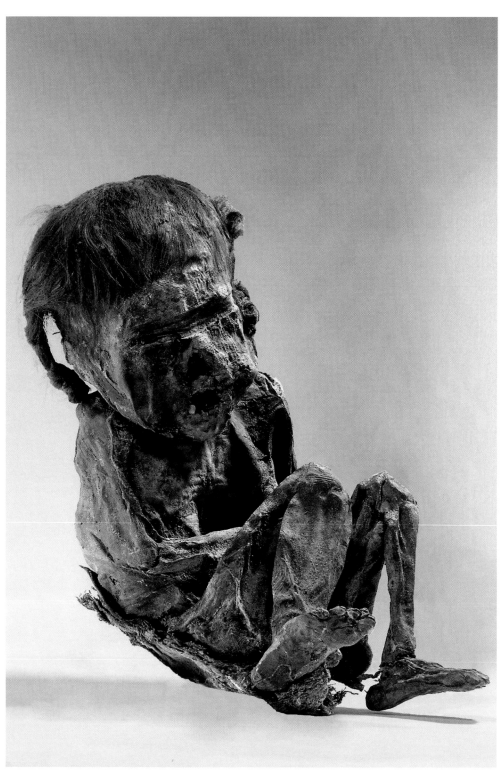

Peruvian child mummy, 1334 AD +/- 42.

Find spot of Juanita's mummy bundle on the Ampato volcano.

Juanita, the Inca mummy from the Andes

On 6 September 1955, the archaeologist and expert for South American mummies Johan Reinhard and his Peruvian colleague Miguel Zárate set off for an expedition to the stratovolcano Ampato (6,288m high) in southern Peru, roughly 100km north-west of Arequipa. At that time the neighbouring volcano Sabancaya was active, which led to a melting of the glacier on the peak of the Ampato and an uncovering of archaeological finds. Two days later, the mountaineers came across a hair ornament made of feathers from the Inca period. Shortly thereafter they discovered a mummy bundle that had evidently fallen down from its original burial place on the peak of the volcano. At closer inspection it became apparent that it was the frozen body of a girl. At that point in time, this was the first frozen female mummy in South America. Johan Reinhard promptly decided

45

Discovery of Juanita.

to bring the 40kg mummy as quickly as possible to Arequipa, since there was a danger that the mummy would be considerably damaged by volcanic ash, and because a reburial was impossible due to the extreme conditions.

With enormous effort, two days later the two scholars reached the Catholic university Santa Maria in Arequipa, where a laboratory under the direction of Professor José Antonio Chávez was immediately set up for the examination of the mummy and measures for its preservation were taken. Reinhard and his colleagues soon returned to the find spot in order to carry out thorough archaeological excavations. In the process further mummies and grave goods were uncovered and documented.

The mummy of the young girl tied into a bundle received the nickname Juanita, derived from the Spanish word for Johan, but she is also called the Ice Maiden, virgin from the ice. The examination of the

Female statuette of gold given as a burial good.

mummy revealed the outer wrapping was probably badly damaged by the fall. In addition, one side of the girl's face shows a darker discolouration. In the mummy bundle were found, among other things, tufts of hair, possibly from her first haircut, a shell on a string and a small cloth bag. In addition, a bag with coca leaves, several cloak pins, small figurines and a vessel containing maize beer and roasted sweetcorn were found.

In May 1996 Juanita was flown to the US for further studies. In the department of radiology of the Johns Hopkins Hospital, Baltimore, she underwent a computed tomographic examination. The examining team detected a fracture above the right eye. It was concluded that she must have received a heavy blow to her right temple, which could possibly have led to her death. Yet it cannot be excluded that the fracture happened post-mortem, i.e. after death, as a consequence of the fall of

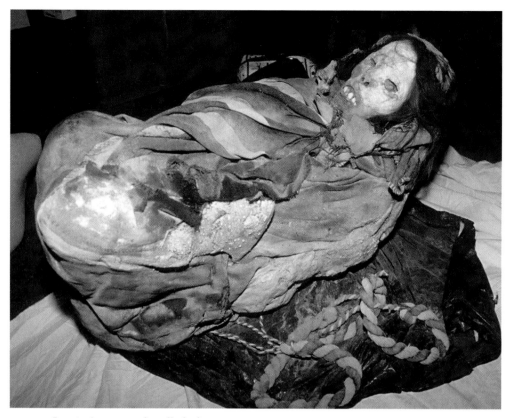

Juanita's mummy bundle before its unwrapping.

the mummy bundle before its discovery. However, we have to assume in any case that the girl found a quick death during the ceremony of sacrifice due to exhaustion, and possibly intoxicated by alcoholic beverages.

An examination of the stomach content with a fine biopsy needle revealed further that Juanita consumed her last, vegetarian meal approximately six to eight hours before her death. Apart from that, the mummy showed no indications of malnutrition or other diseases. Bone structure and bone growth were entirely normal.

The anthropological evaluation revealed that the girl was roughly 14 years old at the time of death and 1.40m tall. Radiocarbon dating of her hair, performed by the University of California in Riverside, revealed that Juanita must have lived 540 years ago, around 1470 AD, thus shortly before Christopher Columbus landed in America. Further investigations yielded results of the pollen of seventeen different plants found in Juanita's clothes. Studies on her genetic make-up helped in the reconstruction of the population history of South America.

In the question of the future preservation of the mummy the specialists agreed that the body should be kept in 100 percent humidity and temperatures around -20°C. For this purpose a specially adapted transport and storage unit was manufactured, which enable a continuous control and regulation of temperature and humidity. Furthermore the construction permitted a viewing of the mummy. This had the result that Juanita became a popular exhibit first in the US and

Juanita in crouched position.

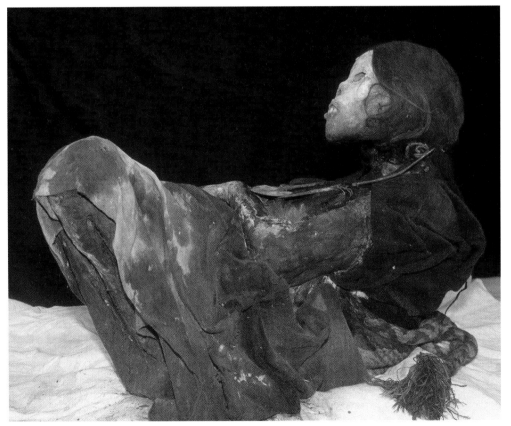

Juanita's hands in detail.

later in Japan. More than 80,000 people admired her in less than a month in the Explorers' Hall of the National Geographic Society alone. In Japan the exhibition toured many different cities in fifteen months. These exhibitions of the virgin from the ice were accompanied by many critical voices, since the frequent transportations in particular represented an increased risk to her preservation.

After the visits abroad Juanita returned to Peru and is shown today in the Museo Santuarios de la Universidad Católica de Santa María in Arequipa, in a cooled display case. Juanita certainly represents an especially well-preserved example of a mummy from the Inca period, who achieved special publicity due to her history of discovery and detailed examination. On the other hand, she is only one specimen of an incredible multitude and variety of mummies offered by South America. We can only hope that after Juanita and some others many more South American mummies will be able to undergo a similarly detailed investigation in order to answer questions concerning the mummification practices, the natural processes of mummification and the respective cultural backgrounds of different societies.

Chinchorro mummies, the earliest artificially preserved mummies

The name Chinchorro is derived from a burial site situated on the coast in Arica (northern Chile). It was discovered in the early twentieth century by Max Uhle and contained an estimated number of 282 artificially made mummies. The eponymous site for the Chinchorro culture was dated 5050 to 500 BC, and hence the interments there represent the earliest records for artificial mummification.

Mummy bundles of the Chinchorro culture.

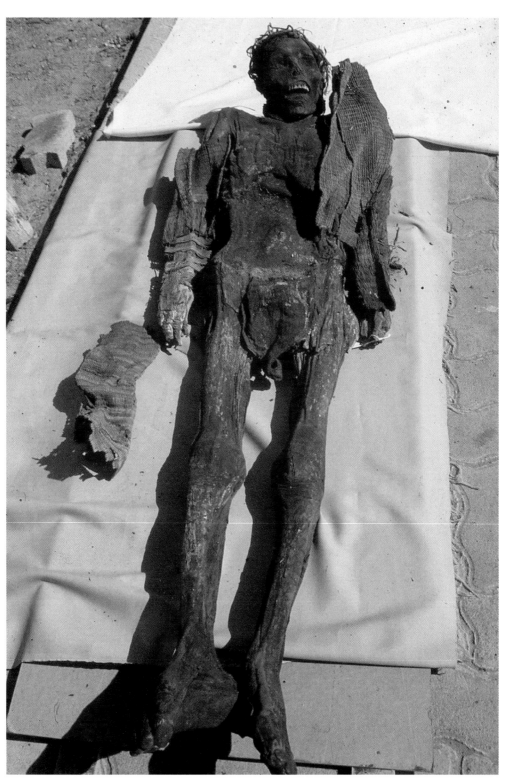

Unwrapped Chinchorro mummy.

The Chinchorro were hunter-gatherers and fishermen who lived along the Pacific coast of the Atamaca Desert from northern Chile to southern Peru. The earliest attestations of the Chinchorro culture come from Acha and date to 7000 BC. Here the earliest corpses, mummified in a natural manner, were also found, for example the so-called Acha Man dating to 7020 BC. Large amounts of discarded shells and isotope examinations of human bones suggest that the proportion of marine food, i.e. fish and seafood, was approximately 90 percent.

Between the earliest attestations for natural mummification dating back to 7020 BC and the beginning of artificial mummification around 5050 BC is a gap of almost 2,000 years. There are no known mummies from this period and it is unclear how exactly the specific form of mummification used by the Chinchorro developed. One theory is that at first a heightened arsenic pollution in water led to high infant mortality. It is known that high natural arsenic contents exist in the Atamaca Desert. The arsenic could have reached the drinking water via the rivers and might have constituted a health risk, especially for the less resilient children. Because of mourning the great loss of children, the community might have decided to preserve their bodies.

After the artificial mummification had been successfully applied to the children it was decided to extend this practice to all other age groups. However, it is not clear if the form of mummification was developed due to an increased infant mortality or gradually during the 2,000 years, for which no records exist. At any rate the mummification practice of the Chinchorro reached an incredibly high complexity that definitely matches the elaborate methods of the ancient Egyptian embalmers, especially considering that the earliest records of artificial mummification in the Chinchorro culture are 2,000 years earlier than the first indications for it in ancient Egypt.

The mummification techniques show a certain change during the course of time. For the most elaborate method initially the skin and muscle tissue as well as the brain were removed from the body, the skeleton was disarticulated and the bones were dried. Subsequently they were re-assembled, the joints reinforced and essential body parts stabilised with sticks. The muscles and soft tissue were replaced with clay and plant components and covered and tied with the original skin or hide. Afterwards the face was covered with a clay mask and adorned

Chinchorro child mummy.

with a wig made of hair. Finally the body surface was completely painted with black manganese. In another variation the body was not disarticulated completely but the organs were removed through several incisions and the body dehydrated. The head was detached to remove the brain, then the body was stuffed with different materials in order to give it a roughly natural shape, and reinforced with sticks. The incisions were sewn up with grass. Finally the body was painted with a red ferric oxide paint apart of the re-attached head. For this reason we speak in this case of the red mummification technique in contrast to the black mummification technique described above.

In the latest mummification method of the Chinchorro culture neither the organs were removed nor incisions made into the body, but the body was merely covered with a thick layer of clay and sand thickened with eggs or fish glue. The bodies were then interred. It is unclear which influences led to the alterations in the mummification techniques, but we may assume that through contact with neighbouring peoples and the introduction of agriculture to the coastal region a change in the mortuary practice took place, which in the end resulted in the disappearance of this very sophisticated and elaborate mummification method.

The examinations on the Chinchorro mummies permitted scientists, such as the renowned and famous mummy researcher Arthur Aufderheide, insights into the state of health and lifestyle of these people. No indications of trepanations were found on the mummies but other than in some cases, artificial deformations of the skull. The general state of health of the population seems to have been relatively good. Some of the buried individuals even reached an age of more than 60. Yet evidence was found for a certain degree of interpersonal violence. Healed skull fractures were found on around 25 percent of

Exposed mummies of the Chinchorro culture.

the mummies. An adult man was killed by two stabbing wounds in the chest, which were probably caused by harpoons. Furthermore, the body of this man showed unhealed skull fractures and injuries to his face.

Mummies from Europe
In contrast to Egypt and South America there exists no longstanding tradition in Europe to preserve the bodies of deceased individuals for eternity. Only in recent history did the custom develop in southern Europe, especially in southern Italy, to inter members of the clergy and other citizens of high standing in catacombs or basements of churches.

At first, spontaneous mummification of those interred took place, promoted by a special microclimate of aridity, constant ventilation and little change in temperatures. From this natural process a new mortuary culture developed in which the possibility of mummification was used deliberately with the aim to preserve the body and to make it accessible to relatives. However, the natural process of mummification was merely enhanced by placing the dead in specific areas of catacombs or crypts in which climatic conditions were very favourable for the preservation of the body. In these dehydration chambers, the so-called colatoi, the corpses were placed onto terracotta pipes above stone basins to enable the drainage of bodily fluids. In other crypts the dead were placed into niches in walls that possessed drainage openings for the same purpose. The mummification was further supported by an external treatment of the body, for instance by washing with vinegar and insertion of plants and herbs into existing orifices.

From this initially natural then natural-intentional method of mummification the embalming of deceased persons by heavy metallic solutions and, later, formalin developed in the nineteenth century. These techniques found use in the mummification of famous personalities, for example Lenin, Mao Zedong and Evita Perón. In contrast to more modern mummies, the earlier European cultures predominantly include examples of natural mummification.

The best-known representative of natural mummies in Europe is the man from the ice, the glacial mummy from the southern Alps who

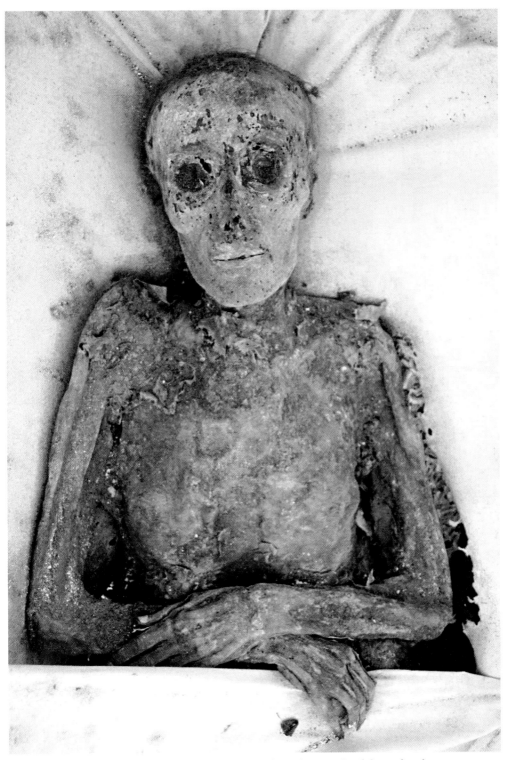

Crypt mummy: Lady Schenck von Geyern from the von Crailsheim family crypt in Sommersdorf Castle.

Bog body of the Tollund Man.

caused a world-wide sensation under his nickname Ötzi. All the details and the latest research results will follow in the next chapter.

Further well-known European mummies are the bog bodies dating to different periods that were preserved naturally in the moorlands of northern Europe. Examples of this natural mummification method are found in north-west Europe, in particular Denmark, northern Germany, the Netherlands, Great Britain and Ireland. Famous examples are the Tollund Man and the Grauballe Man in Denmark, who both died violently to be subsequently buried in the moor.

The acidic characteristics of the moor have led to an extremely good state of preservation of the outer soft tissue, whereas only rubber-like remains of the bones survived. A similar fate befell the man of Neu Versen found in Lower Saxony who was given the nickname Red Francis due to his conspicuous hair. The man died by having his throat cut. From England comes the famous Lindow Man, who was subject of detailed scientific studies.

The excellently preserved bodies in combination with numerous clues to violence stimulated the imagination of scientists and of the public in almost equal measure. This led to some misjudgements culminating in the description of bog body finds without secure provenances. Due to a critical review the number of secure finds of bog bodies is now reduced to approximately 1,000. An example of a misinterpretation, or rather over-interpretation, is the bog body found in Windeby, in Schleswig-Holstein, which would gain dubious

Bog body Windeby I.

59

celebrity as the girl of Windeby. The mummy was initially identified as a 14-year-old girl and, due to the find circumstances, its hand posture and the later discovery of a male bog body in the immediate vicinity, was labelled as an adulteress who had allegedly been tortured before her death and finally executed together with her lover. Only about fifty years after the discovery, the adulteress theory was toppled by scientific re-examinations.

Firstly, it could be demonstrated by means of radiocarbon dating that both corpses were buried at entirely different periods and could not have had any kind of relationship. Secondly, the study revealed that the Windeby girl was actually a 15 to 17-year-old boy who died in the first century AD. In addition it seems to have been a simple but regular burial, as it is indicated by the adjacent pottery vessels and a blanket of grass.

Ötzi, the man from the ice

Since its discovery on 19 September 1991 by Erika and Helmut Simon, the world-famous glacial mummy Ötzi has occupied the public and the media, but also in particular a multitude of scientists who attempt with more and more sophisticated methods to draw the last secrets out of the man from the ice. The application of the most modern examination techniques represent a general trend in mummy studies. Hereby the question arises whether merely historical aspects of the life and death of people of earlier periods can be illuminated by this, or whether these examinations have relevance for modern science too.

The aim of the Ötzi research is not only to collect and critically review all existing

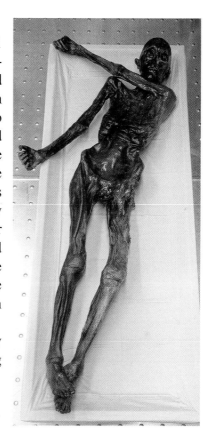

Full-body photo of the Iceman.

Find spot of the Iceman (red circle) at the foot of the Similaun glacier.

objects, sample materials and scientific publications so far, but rather to develop new research approaches in order to get to the last remaining secrets of the infamous mummy. In spite of intensive research since his discovery on the Hauslab Ridge in the Ötztal Alps there still exist unanswered questions concerning the life of the man from the ice and especially his violent death.

Nevertheless the research of the last twenty years has yielded some verified findings on his person and his biography. With the aid of the radiocarbon method, the mummy was dated to 3350 to 3100 BC. This corresponds in the Alpine region to the terminal Neolithic or Chalcolithic period, as the find of an axe with a copper blade with the mummy supports. Isotope studies of various elements, as for example strontium, lead and oxygen, have shown that Ötzi lived south of the main crest of the Alps. The analyses revealed that he spent his early childhood in the upper Eisack valley or the lower Puster valley, and

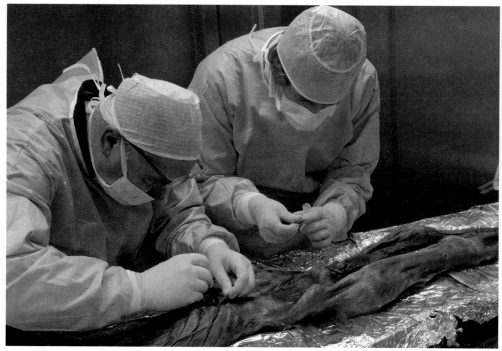

Examination and sample-taking of Ötzi.

that before his death he lived for at least ten years in the Vinschgau. The age determination on the basis of anthropological and histological criteria showed that he must have died at an age of between 40 and 50.

The man from the ice was approximately 160cm tall during his lifetime and weighed around 60kg. He suffered from mild osteoarthritis of the spine, of the knee joints and of the ankles. Parasite eggs of the whipworm were detected in samples from his intestines. On his body numerous tattoos are found in the form of simple strokes that, as a rule, are arranged in parallel with only the right knee showing a cruciform tattoo. These tattoos are almost exclusively found at places where pain must have afflicted the man again and again, especially the lower back, the knees and the ankles. Therefore the suspicion suggests that the stroke-like incisions into the skin were made for therapeutic purposes, either as a form of acupuncture or as

Tattoos on Ötzi's body.

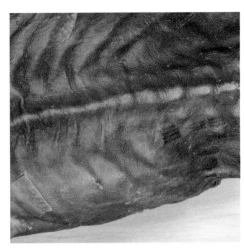

*Detail of the back
showing stroke-like
tattoos in parallel.*

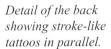

*Tattoo on the back
in normal light.*

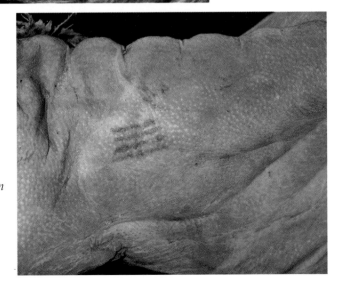

*Tattoo on the back in
ultraviolet light.*

scarification, as it is still used by some people for the therapy of various diseases, for example the Dagomba in Ghana.

It was already suspected that Ötzi did not die a natural death after an arrowhead was discovered in his body in July 2001. Yet this is certain due to a fresh computed tomographic examination in 2005, which clearly showed that the arrow punctured a large blood vessel when penetrating the body and must have caused death within minutes. As a consequence it is confirmed that Ötzi was shot by an arrow directly at the place where he was found more than 5,300 years later. But who was his killer and why was he shot from behind in the high mountain region?

This is probably the earliest criminal case in history and was, and still is, material for many new stories and theories. These can be added to the already existing and partly very outlandish attempts to explain the demise of the man from the ice. Unfortunately, many lack a scientific foundation or are based on disputable examination results.

The Institute for Mummies and the Iceman have therefore made it our task to subject such scientifically questionable papers to a critical review and to carry out new studies with the most modern methods in order to obtain substantiated knowledge of the man from the ice. These do not only concern the background of his violent death but aim to learn more about the person who grew up and lived in this region south of the Alpine main crest.

Ultimately the question arises as to where the man from the ice stands in relation to the population living in southern Tirol today. Is he a direct ancestor, and which information does he carry within himself that could provide us with insights into the occurrence and development of genetically based diseases? These issues are investigated with the most modern examination methods from the various spheres of medicine, palaeogenetics right up to nanotechnology. Care has been taken to use primarily destruction-free examination methods, for which no sample material has to be taken. In some cases this could not be avoided completely, however, as microbiological or genetic studies can only be carried out directly on tissue samples. Fortunately nowadays the smallest amounts are sufficient for biomedical analyses so that no major interference has to take place.

The violent death of the man from the ice

The question of the violent death of the man from the ice exercises a particular fascination and the resulting discussion, in which facts and conjectures often form an entangled web, is led and followed among experts and the wider public with great interest. Therefore it is necessary to approach this question in an almost criminological fashion in order to gather scientifically verifiable facts and to use these for a possible reconstruction of the progression of events.

An important window on the reconstruction of the last hours or days in the life of the iceman is provided by the injuries on his body. Several years ago, a number of wounds to his hand and back were discovered during a thorough inspection. These consisted of a deep cut to the right hand, smaller bruises on the back and the entrance wound of an arrow located in the area to the left shoulder. As a first step, these wounds were the subject of a detailed histological examination, in which micron-thin tissue sections were made, stained and evaluated under the microscope.

In order to be better able to judge the state of preservation of the tissue and to receive possible clues for traces of blood, additional examinations with nanotechnological methods were carried out. Interestingly, the histological staining revealed that the cut to the hand was already at least two or three days old and could not have been inflicted immediately before his death. In contrast, the arrow wound showed no signs of healing and confirmed the already suspected immediate demise of the iceman caused by this injury. Nevertheless a certain connection between the two injuries cannot be entirely excluded, as the injury to the hand might point, for instance, to a longer lasting conflict during which Ötzi's hand was initially injured and he was then fatally wounded by his rival several days later.

In the course of further investigations using nanotechnological procedures a particularly important result could be achieved. Through the use of a so-called atomic force microscope, which enables the examination of tissue samples of nanometre size, first of all an excellent state of preservation of the iceman's tissue structure could be demonstrated. Furthermore, blood in the form of red blood cells could be attested for the first time since the mummy's discovery. The red blood cells showed themselves to be absolutely identical in size

The arrow's point of entry.

and form to modern, fresh erythrocytes. They merely lost some of their elasticity during the 5,000 years within ice and have become slightly soft in comparison to modern samples.

With the help of the Raman spectroscope used during the nanotechnological examination, evidence for fibrin could be found in the back wound. This protein is formed during the early stages of healing and helps to close the wound. In the course of further healing the fibrin is in turn replaced by other substances. With the attestation of fibrin in the back wound it could be confirmed that the man did not long survive the arrow shot but must have died immediately.

Traces of blood on clothing and equipment

Already in 1998 the late Australian scientist Tom Loy published a popular scientific study in which he claimed to have found clear traces of blood on the dagger and axe of the iceman. In subsequent years alleged genetic examinations of these traces were added that allowed Loy to conclude that, before his death, Ötzi was involved in a bloody fight with several opponents that finally cost him his life. This story was spectacularly presented in a documentary produced by the Discovery Channel. The confirmation of the examination results, however, failed to materialise in the form of a scientific publication, which led to justifiable doubts among fellow specialists.

This circumstance was used as an opportunity to carry out a renewed examination of clothing and equipment of the iceman for traces of blood. Besides the question of credibility of previous analyses, the issue should also be addressed to which extent and how much blood seeped from the arrow wound. This is of great importance for the reconstruction of the exact circumstances of death, as the iceman must have experienced severe blood loss through the injury to the artery.

As part of this project, which took place in collaboration with forensic specialists of the Ludwig-Maximilians-University Munich, the clothing and gear of the iceman were systematically screened for blood by means of a special trace lamp and chemical testing strips. With the aid of a forensic lamp it was possible to render discolourations visible on the materials, which indicate blood traces, by employing light of different wave lengths (ultraviolet to visible light). These discolourations cannot as a rule be detected – or hardly so – under normal light conditions.

In a further step the suspect spots were investigated with the help of highly sensitive testing strips that react to the ring structure of haemoglobin. In the case of a clear reaction of the testing strip the existence of blood remnants is considered proven. Remarkably no evidence of blood was revealed on the tools (axe, dagger) during initial

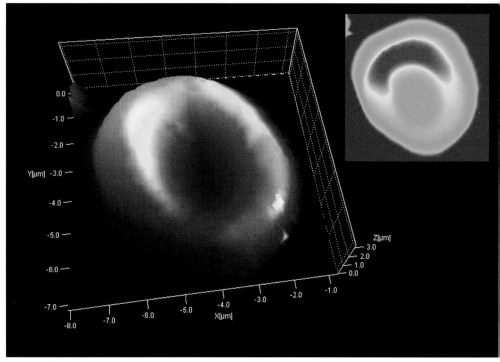

Image created by nanotechnology of a red blood cell of the Iceman.

examinations. Therefore the earlier assertions of Tom Loy could not be confirmed.

Several traces of blood were found on the grass mat and on the fur coat of the iceman. This might be blood that has seeped from the arrow wound. In further examinations it has now to be clarified whether this is actually human blood and whether it comes from the iceman or has to be ascribed to another source.

New finds

With the repeated analysis of the glacial mummy's radiographs new evidence could be gathered. For instance, it was shown that the right upper arm is broken, but that this is probably due to the haphazard recovery. Furthermore, signs of a chronic surplus load in the area of the knee joints were found. From this it can be concluded that the iceman probably spent a lot of time in the mountains and was used to travel in the Alpine region. Probably the most exciting find, however, was the identification of Ötzi's stomach, which was – contrary to earlier assumptions – filled with the remains of food. Earlier attempts at the University of Innsbruck to localise the stomach and to gain the stomach content endoscopically probably failed due to the relatively high and oblique position of the organ behind the rib cage. The fact that the iceman consumed food shortly before his death shines an entirely new light on events at the Hauslaub ridge several thousand years ago. It now seems highly unlikely that he was in a great rush and, for instance, on the run from pursuers. Rather he probably thought himself safe, took a break after a laborious ascent and partook a filling meal. Shortly after he was murdered from an ambush a few metres from his resting place.

The find situation and also the position of the mummy speak clearly for the fact that the iceman died directly at the find spot and was hardly moved, if at all, in the 5,000 years until his discovery. Contrary theories that see evidence for Ötzi's burial at the foot of the Similaun mountain could so far not bear a critical scientific review.

As these results show, the course of events and some circumstances in connection with the killing of the iceman can be progressively reconstructed with the help of scientific examinations. Future analyses and new procedures will certainly add to the clarification of further details concerning this case. Nevertheless, there are also questions, which will be very difficult to answer. Some facts will possibly remain forever lost in the mists of time. Who murdered the iceman and what was the motive of the deed? Was it an act of revenge, or was the cause the rivalry of several groups or even a war-like territorial dispute? Even if these questions can perhaps never be answered definitely, they add to the fascination of the Ötzi case. A certain measure of speculation and ventured theories should be by all means regarded as legitimate, at least as long as these remain strictly separated from substantiated scientific evidence.

Recently efforts were made to develop new research approaches concerning the man from the ice. In large-scale projects the fundamental issue of preservation and of genetic origin and characterisation of the glacial mummy were addressed. Especially with the application of the most modern examination methods, mummy studies were able to build a bridge to modern biological and medical areas of research.

An important question occupying the researchers around Ötzi and other mummies for many years is to what extent life could still exist within the glacial mummy in the form of micro-organisms (bacteria, fungi). Although strict regulations ensure that sterile conditions prevail in the cold storage cell and that the mummy has been free from external microbiological contamination for years, nevertheless it cannot be disregarded that germs are present within the mummy, the growth of which could be triggered by an alteration of the preservation conditions. In particular it is conceivable that cryophilic or cold-adapted bacteria found their way into the mummy during its millennia-long sojourn in snow and ice.

Although currently no evident hazard for the mummy and no visible sign for bacterial activity exist, it is considered very important to scientifically investigate this possibility in order to ensure the long-term survival of this important mummy. The aim of the project is therefore the determination of the presence and variety of bacteria, and here in particular cryophilic micro-organisms, in the man from the ice. These shall be detected through studies of tissue samples from the external and internal parts of the mummified body. The detailed analysis of the micro-organisms takes place in a combination of different methodological approaches, which contain both genetic studies and traditional microbiological procedures. These processes enable a direct verification of micro-organisms.

Another methodological approach is the attestation of metabolic activity of micro-organisms with the aid of mass spectrometric procedures. This highly sensitive technique permits the quantification of gasiform molecules up to an area of 10^{-9} gram. This means that even the smallest traces of bacterial metabolic activity can be detected. Ultimately the study shall extend the state of information on cryophilic micro-organisms that possibly form colonies on the mummy and might lead to middle- to long-term damage. It shall determine their influence on the degradation of organic material of the glacial mummy and develop a strategy that allows preservation in as ideal conditions as possible and, thus, a long-term protection of the mummy.

The genes of the iceman

In recent years the mitochondrial DNA of the iceman was successfully analysed by a team from the University of Camerino in Italy. This genetic material, which derives from certain cell organelles and is only passed on by the mother to her progeny, has shown that Ötzi belongs to a specific genetic group still found in the European region today. Yet he apparently belongs to a subgroup that could not be detected in any modern population so far. This led to the slightly exaggerated interpretation that the iceman originates clearly from the European region, but that no living relatives of his exist today.

However, it has to be taken into account that in such an analysis only the maternal relatives are incorporated and that in addition only a very small segment of the modern population has been genetically studied so far. Relatives of the paternal line are not covered by this method.

It was therefore necessary for a more exact determination of the iceman's genetic roots to carry out as exhaustive an analysis as possible on the entire genetic make-up, i.e. on the nuclear DNA. The greatest problem here lies in the fact that the genetic material has been considerably degraded over the past 5,300 years, or rather has disintegrated into many small fragments. This ancient DNA has to be treated with particular care and in a specially equipped laboratory.

As a consequence a bone sample of the iceman submitted to a DNA extraction during a current project in the laboratory for ancient DNA of the Institute for Mummies and the Iceman. The genetic material obtained subsequently underwent a comprehensive genome sequencing in collaboration with the University of Tübingen and the Saarland University of Homburg. In this ultramodern procedure the entire genetic information from a single sample is duplicated and evaluated in several steps. The Life Technologies company (US) provided the latest platform (SOLiD 4) for the precious Ötzi sample, which was not available on the market at that time. The first appraisal of the sequencing results revealed an astonishingly good state of preservation for the nuclear DNA of the iceman.

With the aid of bio-informatic analyses a coverage of roughly 85 percent of Ötzi's genome could be reconstructed. It has to be emphasised, however, that a chromosomal genome consists of about 3,000,000 base pairs and contains considerably more information as the mitochondrial genome with merely 17,000 base pairs. This result is of immense importance as the genetic make-up contains all genes that characterise the iceman, his body functions and also his potential diseases.

The analysis of the genetic information provided detailed knowledge of Ötzi's appearance and body functions, his origin and ancestry as well as clues to diseases and predispositions for such. For instance, the genetic examination showed that Ötzi had brown eyes (95 percent probability) and not blue ones, as had been assumed so far. In addition he was lactose-intolerant, i.e. he could not digest milk sugar. It has to be pointed out that probably the majority of the then population was not yet capable of digesting lactose. The genetic mutation resulting in lactose tolerance turned out to be advantageous in the course of the development of husbandry and agriculture, but only won through over many generations, and it took roughly until the Middle Ages for the European population to become lactose tolerant.

Another surprising result of the genetic analysis was that the iceman carried some genetically inherent predispositions which, under specific circumstances, could have led to serious illnesses. In particular Ötzi showed a heightened risk of cardiac disease and a circulatory disorder, which might have made him prone to heart attacks and stroke, had he not died prematurely of an arrow shot.

An examination of the entire genetic make-up also permitted an analysis of the Y-chromosome, i.e. the male sex chromosome, which reflects the male relational line and allows statements about the population affiliation and origin. It was shown that the iceman belonged to a very rare haplogroup, which is today encountered rarely in Europe. Only on Corsica and Sardinia is Ötzi's group still represented relatively frequently. From this it can be concluded that the iceman and the population on Sardinia and Corsica had common ancestors who immigrated to Europe during the Neolithic period.

In wide parts of Europe the representatives of this group were superseded in the course of time and only in remote regions such as the Mediterranean islands could they survive in greater numbers until today. The question to which extent these populations have also survived in isolated areas of the Alps, and if living relatives of the iceman in the widest sense still reside in southern Tirol, cannot be

72

Reconstruction of the Iceman.

currently answered due to a lack of data. However, this is the topic of a current research project of the EURAC Institute for Mummies and the Iceman.

In order to extract additional information from this comprehensive data set, further very complex and time-consuming analyses are necessary. Results so far already demonstrate that the possibility exists to obtain an array of hitherto hidden information on the iceman. Initially an exact genetic fingerprint can be made of Ötzi on the basis of the existing data and the question of his exact origin and of the existence of living relatives can be addressed. Furthermore, different genes can be studied, which have defined his appearance but also provide clues on diseases or predispositions to such. The question will be especially exciting as to which extent genetic differences between ancient and modern populations can be discerned.

Numerous diseases widespread today, such as diabetes, Alzheimer's, atherosclerosis and cardiac diseases, have an important genetic background that increasingly come into the spotlight of modern medical studies. The decoded genome of the iceman offers a unique opportunity to gain an insight into the situation 5,000 years ago and to understand if and to what extent these genetic mutations occurred. If indeed such specific mutations can be detected in the genetic make-up of the iceman it has to be seriously questioned whether these diseases are so-called diseases of civilisation.

In principle it should be noted that a better understanding of the evolution of diseases and their genetic foundation forms an important basis for the development of new approaches to treatment and strategies of prevention. Our genetic examinations of the glacial mummy definitely have great potential to make an important contribution to this.

Rosalia Lombardo and the Capuchin crypt in Palermo

In 1534, Capuchin monks established themselves in Palermo. To this end they received permission to erect their monastery next to the already existing church Santa Maria della Pace on the outskirts of the city. Just as the Franciscans did, the Capuchins venerated their dead, who remained present in day-to-day life by means of prayers and memorials.

At this time the departed monks were buried in large pits in the environs of the church. As no burials were allowed within the church according to the founder's charter of the order, the constitutions were accepted in 1536 in the monastery of Saint Euphemia in Rome.

At the end of the sixteenth century forty-five well-preserved corpses were discovered during an accidental exhumation. This find was seen as a direct interference by God and thereupon it was decided that the bodies should be kept in a different area. According to historical sources, in 1599 forty of the forty-five mummified corpses, among them Silvestro da Gubbio, were transferred to a new room erected behind the main altar.

Frate Silvestre da Gubbio.

Due to the increasing number of Capuchins living and dying in the convent, an additional room and a chapel were set up in 1601. Thus the first corridor of a subterranean tomb complex for the Capuchin monks came into being in 1619, which later became known as the Capuchin crypt or catacombs. Around 1680 the corridor reached the area around the main altar and the monks buried there were included.

Today the mummy of Silvio da Gubbio can be admired as the oldest mummy of the Capuchin crypt in the immediate vicinity of the entrance.

During the sixteenth century the first noblemen sponsoring the Capuchin monks were accepted into the catacombs. Already in 1732 the crypt had reached its modern extent with four corridors in a square layout. Indeed, the demand for an interment in the catacombs of Palermo was so great until 1787 that the subterranean tomb complex was made accessible for everyone. After 1823 this vast and extraordinary subterranean cemetery was completely occupied and only repairs and maintenance were carried out thereafter.

Corridor in the catacombs with numerous mummies.

Details of some mummies.

Today more than 1,800 mummies are kept in the Capuchin crypt, the majority of which are lying flat or hanging from hooks in the wall niches along the corridors. The other corpses are found in wooden coffins, partly beautifully wrought and decorated. In the course of time the departed were arranged according to sex, age and profession, so that essentially five main areas came into being for monks, priests, various professional groups, women and children. The mummies are almost all clothed and wear hats, shoes and occasionally even gloves. Some of the mummified monks also show crowns of thorns and ropes around their necks as signs of repentance.

It may seem strange that such a preservation of the departed was practised in Palermo. Yet this phenomenon can also be observed in numerous other churches and crypts of Sicily and southern Italy. In the Early Modern Era this form of interment was applied first to the representatives of the churches and congregations and later extended to nobles and upper-class citizens, who were willing to exhibit their bodies permanently. Allegedly this served to strengthen the social elites and their perpetuation.

Shortly after death the corpses were brought to preparation rooms and laid out on special installations, for example onto grills made out of terracotta pipes above stone basins or stone seats with openings that allowed for the drainage of body fluids and, hence, amplified the natural process of mummification. Then the cell-like rooms, called colatoi, were closed for the duration of roughly a year. Afterwards the dried corpses were taken out, washed with vinegar and finally dressed and exhibited or placed into coffins. In cases where mummification was not entirely successful and the body had become largely skeletonised, the missing soft tissue was replaced with straw.

Until today the processes taking place in the dehydration rooms have not been verified by experiments. However, it can be assumed that in rooms dug into the volcanic rock, relatively low humidity and constantly cool temperatures prevailed that influenced the mummification process favourably.

Details of some mummies.

Besides the intentional but naturally occurring process of mummification, however, examples for an artificial mummification practice, also called embalming, are found too, in the catacombs of Palermo. Already in earlier periods during epidemics the dead were dipped in or sprinkled with lime, a substance with strongly dehydrating characteristics. In the early nineteenth century various methods were developed to preserve corpses. These partly encompassed the opening of the body for organ removal or the direct application of embalming substances, the dipping of the entire body in a mummification solution, or the direct injection of the embalming substance into a large blood vessel.

An important pioneer of the arterial injection was the Italian Giuseppe Tranchina, who developed this method in the 1830s and made the removal of internal organs superfluous. With his newly developed technique several historically important personalities were mummified, among them Queen Maria Christina of Savoy (1836). At this time the embalming substances were mainly composed of mercury or arsenic solutions, which were never prohibited by Italian law in spite of their high toxicity. In addition vermilion, a mercury sulphite, and red lead, a lead oxide, were used as colorants to give the deceased a true-to-life complexion. The use of glass eyes and make-up was equally a frequent practice.

Despite the development of these procedures for the artificial preservation of the departed the interments in the catacombs were soon to find their end. Shortly after the national unification of Italy in 1861 the dehydration of corpses was prohibited on the basis of hygienic considerations. New cemeteries were established and a burial outside these areas was no longer permitted. The Capuchin crypt was still used for another sixty years, but only as a temporary repository for coffins before the actual interment in the nearby cemetery. The latest identified coffin in the catacombs belongs to Giovanni Licata di Baucina, Count of Isnello, who passed away in the year 1939.

Among the last interments in the catacombs are mummies that were prepared by Alfredo Salafia, a local taxidermist and embalmer, who at the beginning of the twentieth century developed a new method for the long-term preservation of human tissue apparently free from toxic chemicals. Among them are the mummies of the American vice-consul

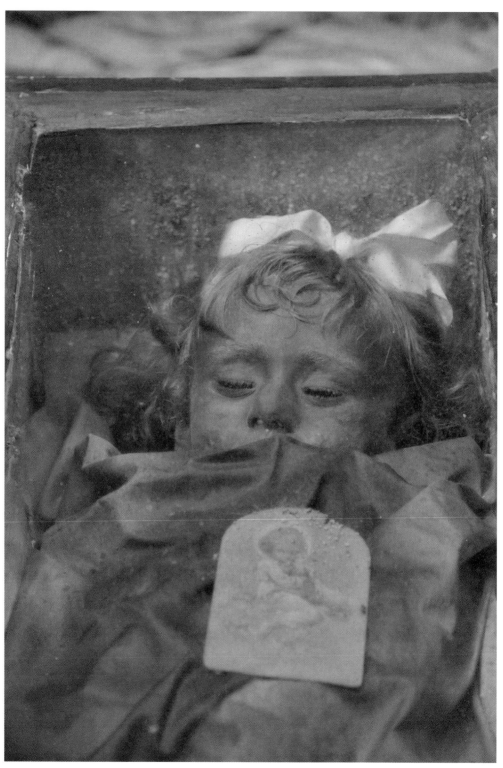

Mummy of Rosalia Lombardo.

Giovanni Paterniti (1911), Ernesto Salafia, a famous fencer of his times (1914), and the little girl Rosalia Lombardo (1920), who is also known as 'sleeping beauty' due to her extraordinary state of preservation.

Rosalia Lombardo was born on 13 December 1918 as the daughter of the officer Mario Lombardo (1890-1980) and Maria Di Cara (1897-1966), and she died on 6 December 1920, only a week before her second birthday. According to the autopsy report she died of bronchial pneumonia. Her parents decided to let their daughter be embalmed by Alfredo Salafia. Salafia's newly developed procedure consisted of a single injection with the embalming substance, preferably into the femoral artery, which penetrated the body with the aid of gravity. The exact composition of the fluid was kept secret during Salafia's life and was only be uncovered a few years ago by the Institute for Mummies and the Iceman's project. One of my colleagues, Darlo Piombino-Mascali, found a manuscript written by Alfredo Salafia that contained the detailed description of the formula. The embalming solution is composed of one part glycerine, one part formalin saturated with zinc sulphate and zinc chloride, and one part alcohol saturated with salicylic acid. Therefore Salafia has to be viewed as one of the first to use a solution on the basis of formaldehyde, which gradually replaced the heavy metal solutions used so far. In addition, Salafia describes in his manuscript the use of paraffin wax dissolved in ether, which was injected under the facial skin of the deceased in order to let the features appear plump and more life-like. The mummy of Rosalia Lombardo is still exhibited in the Capuchin crypt today in its original coffin, which is closed with a glass cover. Only her head is visible while the rest of her body is covered with a cloth. Her face and hair, decorated with a yellow ribbon, show an impressive state of preservation that indeed recalls a sleeping rather than a deceased girl. Recently, however, symptoms of deterioration of the mummy have increased. For example, the hair and textiles seem paler than in earlier photos, while the face has become darker and less plump.

A radiological examination carried out by our institute has shown that not only the head but the entire body of Rosalia Lombardo is preserved. On digital X-ray images the internal organs, for example the brain and the liver, were recognisable too. During a further

The modern glass case with Rosalia Lombardo's mummy.

examination we had the opportunity to study the little girl in a mobile CT scanner, which solely for this purpose was transported to the Capuchin monastery in Palermo mounted on a special lorry. During the computer-based tomographic inspection the extraordinarily good preservation of virtually all internal organs was demonstrated. Additionally, pneumonia was diagnosed and thus the cause of death originally attested confirmed. Furthermore it was possible to gain a more detailed insight into the sequence of the mummification process and the distribution of the embalming substance via the blood vessels.

Due to the worsening of the state of Rosalia Lombardo's mummy and the currently unfavourable climatic conditions in the Capuchin crypt – which are decidedly too humid – we resolved to design a new concept for her preservation. The aim was to transfer the mummy into an environment with constant, controlled humidity, and free from oxygen. Excessive humidity in general presents a great threat to mummies, as through this processes of decomposition and putrefaction resume and, in the worst cases, can lead to complete destruction of the mummy. In addition, the oxygen existing in the regular atmosphere promotes the growth of many bacteria and fungi that can cause significant damage, especially in a humid setting.

Modern concepts of preservation regarding biological materials therefore aim in principle for relatively low humidity and an oxygen-free atmosphere, whereby the latter might be saturated with nitrogen or an inert gas such as argon. In the case of Rosalia Lombardo we developed a completely new display cabinet, which should guarantee optimal preservation but also good visibility of the mummy. After all, the little girl's mummy represents probably the most famous treasure of the Capuchin crypt and should remain accessible to visitors of the catacombs.

Another important aspect was to develop a passive system needing little or no maintenance, as in the convent there are no adequate personnel at hand who can carry out a permanent control and maintenance of the installation.

The cabinet, which is already operating, consists of a high-grade steel frame covered with a convex double glass sheet with inbuilt UV protection sealed air-tight with special wax. The humidity was adjusted to the calculated ideal value by means of valves, and the interior of the cabinet filled with nitrogen until the oxygen was completely replaced. By means of wireless sensors connected to a computer the values can now be controlled and, so far, have remained stable.

Thus Rosalia Lombardo could be saved from the threat of deterioration for now. Nevertheless the climatic situation in the catacombs remains inadequate for a permanent preservation of the mummies resting there. Further measures are urgently needed to restore the original favourable temperature and humidity, as otherwise heavy damage to the unique collection has to be feared. We can only hope that the necessary financial resources will be provided and that the Capuchin monks, the authorities responsible such as the

Monuments Office in Palermo, and the scientists involved will find a solution to preserve this important and interesting cultural heritage.

Church mummies from the crypt in Vác, Hungary
Although many mummies are found in the vaults, crypts and catacombs of churches in southern Italy and Sicily, this phenomenon is by no means restricted to Italy or the south of Europe. Especially in the German-speaking region numerous crypts are found from the sixteenth century onwards, in which wealthy citizens were interred in the church environment, particularly crypts of rulers and the nobility in which high-ranking personalities found their final resting place. Examples for this are in the Capuchin crypt in Vienna, where the rulers from the house of Habsburg were buried for many generations, and the crypt in St Michael's church, in which roughly 4,000 wealthy citizens and noblemen were interred. In Germany, for instance, in Quedlinburg we find in the crypt of the monastery church St Servatius the mummified remains of King Henry I and his wife Mathilde, and in the princely crypt the mummies of historically well-known personalities such as Countess Aurora of Königsmarck and Marie Elisabeth of Schleswig-Holstein-Gottorf.

Another good example is the family crypt of the house of Crailsheim in Sommersdorf near Ansbach, in which the family's ancestors were interred and became naturally mummified. The German Mummy Project of the Reiss-Engelhorn Museum in Mannheim under the direction of Dr Wilfried Rosendahl is carrying out a scientific study on this family crypt and is focusing in general on the phenomenon of church and crypt mummies throughout Europe.

A particularly interesting find context exists in the so-called lead cellar of the St Petri minster in Bremen. Here naturally mummified corpses were discovered in the nineteenth century in the minster's eastern crypt. After it had been assumed for a long time that lead used for roof repairs stored in the crypt led to the preservation of the interred, it was in the meantime demonstrated by measurements that this could not have been the reason and that rather the favourable climatic conditions typical for churches were the decisive factor.

The fascination emanating from the lead cellar mummies has, however, led to thrilling stories being told about the dead and the circumstances of their demise. For instance, one of the mummies is allegedly a roof tiler who died through a fall and was only found many years later in his mummified state. Yet recent examinations brought to light that the body does not show corresponding injuries, but has a bullet stuck in the back. Therefore he is more likely a soldier who probably died in the war against the Swedes. Neither could the stories about the mummy of an English lady and that of a student be verified.

There are numerous other examples for church mummies in Europe, from Spain and France, by way of Norway and Lithuania, to Poland, the Czech Republic and Croatia. In some of these cases it has been possible to subject these mummies to a detailed scientific study and thus to gain profound insights into the life and death of the past population. Such an example is represented by the finds in the Dominican church in the Hungarian town of Vác.

The church in Vác, Hungary.

The small town of Vác is situated at the Danube north of Budapest. During restoration works on the Dominican church in 1994 a vast vault with crypt was discovered under the church, which had been forgotten for a long time. Within it researchers found numerous richly decorated coffins stacked to the ceiling and containing the mummified remains of 265 departed souls.

According to historical sources the Dominican church of Vác was erected around 1699 and the construction of the crypt was begun in 1729, in which the first interment took place in 1731 according to the death register. The crypt was used as a burial site in the following years until the beginning of the nineteenth century. A large number of the coffins display inscriptions with the name and death date of the deceased person. By this means the Hungarian researchers were able to identify 166 of the 265 mummies and to obtain, with the help of the death register, further information on age, familial relationships, cause of death and occasionally even the profession of the interred. For instance, the genealogies of entire families and their living conditions more than 200 years ago, which were characterised by numerous illnesses and high infant mortality, could be reconstructed on the basis of the Vác mummies. The 265 mummies are split between 119 male and 107 female individuals, but for thirty-nine persons the gender could no longer be determined. The age span ranges from newborn to 95, and the average life expectancy was 44.6 for men and 38.8 for women. Those who survived the critical childhood phase could on average reach an age of 53 or 54.

Examinations of the teeth revealed that the general state of the natural dentition was evidently much worse in the eighteenth century than in comparative series of earlier periods. Women had worse teeth than men. A lack of dental hygiene of the population at that time led to heavy dental plaque, which is still detectable on the mummies today. Since dental plaque contains protein, carbohydrates and bacteria, dietary habits and even germs can be reconstructed with the help of mummies or skeletal finds. The analysis of the dental plaque on the Vác mummies resulted in evidence of animal food in the form of collagen and muscle tissue, and primarily of wheat, maize and potato starch. This represents the first record of a high proportion of maize and potatoes in the diet of the inhabitants of Vác.

Death register of the Dominican church.

Besides occasional findings on illnesses and causes of death of the deceased individuals, in particular the detection of tuberculosis caused a stir in the scientific world. In a large-scale study, Hungarian scientists under the direction of Ildiko Pap of the Hungarian Museum for Natural History in Budapest and colleagues from Great Britain and Israel, examined the mummies with radiological, histological and molecular biological methods for signs of tuberculosis. It is historically known that tuberculosis was one of the most frequent causes of death in Europe of the nineteenth and twentieth centuries, and that it left epidemic traces throughout Europe. Yet it was not known to what extent the inhabitants of Vác had suffered from this terrible disease and how frequently this ailment occurred there at that time.

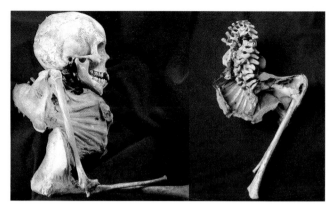

Mummy of Józef Weiskopf showing a severely deformed spine.

The first morphological and radiological examinations of the mummified bodies already brought to light the first cases with advanced bone tuberculosis. In this advanced stage of the disease the pathogen *Mycobacterium tuberculosis*, at first restricted to the lungs, spreads through the entire body and affects the organs, in particular the bones and joints. Typically the spine is preferentially afflicted, which can lead to the formation of a hump through the destruction of individual vertebrae (Pott's disease). In further studies tissue samples were taken from 253 mummies and tested by molecular biological means for the presence of remains of the tuberculosis pathogen. In almost 70 percent of the mummies the genome of the tuberculosis bacteria could be verified. These findings clearly confirm that tuberculosis was very widely spread in Vác at that time, probably all over Hungary too, and that virtually every inhabitant was exposed to the pathogen. Nevertheless, many survived the disease and only died in old age, even though the tubercles are still detectable. Therefore the Vác mummies offer the unique opportunity to study questions of genetic disposition and natural immunity of humans against tuberculosis at a time when there were neither adequate treatments nor antibiotics available.

Such insights are essential to the understanding of the mechanisms of this disease and to the finding of new approaches for treating tuberculosis more efficiently and successfully or avoiding it all together. After all, tuberculosis is still one of the most frequent causes of death world-wide and claims several million victims every year.

Mummy showing the traces of an autopsy.

With the aid of the coffin inscriptions, information from the death register and the medical examinations some special individual cases and finds in Vác could be reconstructed. For instance, four mummies in total showed evidence of autopsies carried out. This suggests that the openings of the corpses were not performed for the purpose of anatomical studies but rather to establish the cause of death, whether due to illness or violence. So-called pathological or forensic autopsies were fairly widespread in eighteenth-century Hungary. On the mummy of a roughly 20-year-old man signs of the autopsy are still clearly visible. The upper torso was cut open with a y-shaped incision, some organs removed and the skull opened too. Most likely the autopsy was carried out for forensic reasons in this case.

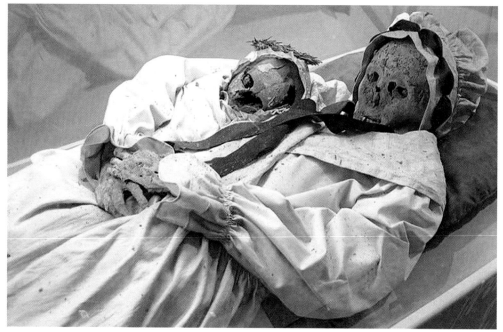

Mummy of Tereszia Borsodi.

On the mummy of Terézia Borsody, who died in 1794 at the age of 26, scientists found clear evidence for a caesarean. Her son was evidently born alive and baptised, but died soon after and was in the end interred with his mother. At that time it was common to carry out post-mortem caesarean sections on mothers already passed away in order to enable the baptism of the child, if it was still alive, and thus to save the soul. The examination of the mummy yielded no anatomical reasons why the child could not be born under normal circumstances. Size and weight of the child also speak for a normal development. Possibly the young mother was incapable to bear the child for health reasons and died before the birth. The post-mortem caesarean enabled the baptism of the child, but could not prevent his death.

Among the mummies of the Dominican church were several nuns who received their final resting place there. One of these nuns had her heart removed after death via a deep incision into the chest, another had two fingers of her left hand cut off and placed in a parcel. The fingers were separated shortly before or after her death, but the reasons for this remain obscure.

In a richly decorated wooden coffin the remains of the nun Baroness Antónia Tauber were found. She came from a noble family

Mummy of a nun.

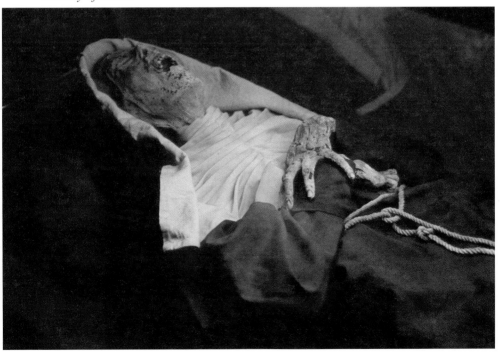

91

and died in 1768 at the age of 37. The very well-preserved mummy exhibits a disfigured face and a very strong deformation of the spine, probably caused by a developmental disorder. In addition, tuberculosis was attested for her too, though it is unclear whether the disease was the cause of death. It is known from historical sources that Antónia Tauber was an excellent teacher for the nobility's youth in spite of her physical defects and she displayed a loving, faithful and friendly disposition.

Lenin and Evita Perón, modern mummies from our time
Lenin, who was actually called Vladimir Ilyich Ulyanov, was born on 22 April 1870 in Simbirsk and died on 21 January 1924 in Gorki. He was a communist politician and one of the theoreticians of scientific socialism. The October revolution initiated by him finally led to the foundation of the Soviet Union. Lenin died at the age of 54, after he had suffered several strokes. Nonetheless the exact cause of Lenin's death has not been definitely resolved until today. Several illnesses

Lenin's embalmed corpse.

92

were debated, such as arteriosclerosis and syphilis, or the consequences of a bullet wound, received during an assassination attempt on 30 August 1918. The death of the Soviet leader posed a great danger to the stability of the emergent Soviet Union as renewed civil war and possibly the collapse of the regime threatened.

In order to maintain the memory of Lenin and his achievements, his successor in office – Joseph Stalin – ordered the embalming of his body. This evidently took place against the will of the departed and his family and also stood in opposition to the ideology of the revolution.

At first the prerequisites for a preservation were favourable, since at the time of death in January sub-zero temperatures prevailed and the corpse could be kept preserved. The pathologist Aleksey Ivanovitch Abrikossov was commissioned for the preservation and injected six litres of a mixture of formalin, alcohol, chlorine, water and glycerine into the body by way of the main artery. However, the treatment showed only temporary success and in the course of time the corpse started to dry up and show signs of decay. Even the cooling of the body could not stop this process, and soon post-mortem lividity, skin discolourations and a gaping of the lips could be observed.

A heated debate about the correct concept of preservation flared up, until finally the experienced embalmer Vladimir Worobjow, director of the institute of anatomy in Kharkov, could be persuaded to lead the embalming. He was assisted by the young biochemist Boris Ilyich Sbarski and the anatomist Peter Karusin.

Meanwhile two months had already passed since the death of Lenin and an urgent need to act arose. Worobjow started immediately with the removal of the internal organs and subsequently washed the cavity with distilled water and vinegar. The tissue was fixed with formalin, and face, hands and torso were wrapped in cotton drenched in a formaldehyde solution. In addition, a rubber basin was acquired, in which Lenin's corpse was immersed in a special solution. This consisted at first of alcohol and glycerine and was then replaced with a mixture of glycerine and water. This was followed by ample quantities of potassium acetate as well as chloroquinine and phenol for disinfection. By way of numerous incisions into the body the liquid was absorbed into the tissue, which regained its previously lost moisture. Additionally various cosmetic treatments were carried out in order to remove unattractive stains and to let the skin appear rosy. The eyeballs were replaced with prosthetics and the lips and eyes sewn shut in an invisible manner. By these means the individual facial features could be preserved and an appealing portrait created from the corpse.

In spite of the elaborate mummification of Lenin constant maintenance and after-care is still necessary today. Twice a week the exposed body parts are brushed with embalming fluid and every eighteen months the body is thoroughly inspected and immersed into the bath described above. Stains or mouldy spots are regularly removed and cosmetically touched up during this process. Equally the clothing has to be regularly washed and renewed.

The mausoleum in which Lenin is resting and in which the department for the preservation is located was at first – immediately after his death – erected from oak wood on Red Square in Moscow. A second wooden mausoleum was replaced in 1930 by a pyramid-like construction of reddish brown granite and labradorite. The integrated research centre has numerous scientists with the assignment to protect the mummy from decay and to further study the brain of the deceased in detail. It was assumed that the genius of the leader of the revolution could be detected in the brain structure.

During the Second World War Stalin ordered the transfer of the mummified corpse to Tyumen in western Siberia. The accompanying scientists used the time to carry out a thorough overhaul of the embalming and to give the corpse an almost life-like complexion. The manner of preservation has led to repeated doubts of the authenticity of the exhibited mummy and to the suspicion that there is a wax model of Lenin in the glass coffin. This theory can not be refuted completely, but those experts who have seen the mummy close-up are of the opinion that this is not a replica.

With the end of the Soviet Union the mausoleum lost its importance, and the emerging Russian state was no longer willing to raise the considerable funds for the preservation and the operation of the research laboratory. In 1990 the mausoleum was declared a World Cultural Heritage by UNESCO and is currently supervised by only a small group of scientists who still guarantee Lenin's preservation. In order to finance the laboratory, external commissions are now accepted, for which corpses are prepared for interment with the aid of the preservation methods tested on Lenin.

Another equally impressive example of the mummification of a historically significant person, whose body should not be abandoned to decay, is Eva Perón, also known as Evita. The second wife of the Argentinian dictator Juan Perón died a slow, agonising death on 26 July 1953 at the age of only 33.

Already during her life Eva Perón was ardently admired by her people, based on her fairytale-like rise, her charm and her beauty. Her tragic death led to a martyr-like veneration and public mourning reached unbelievable dimensions. During the lying in state of the deceased lady, in a coffin with a glass lid in the hall of congress, lasting twelve days, allegedly 12,000,000 mourners said farewell to her.

It was necessary to embalm Evita's body for the long farewell ceremony. This was taken on by the experienced embalmer and physician Pedro Ara, who at that time was cultural attaché to the Spanish embassy in Argentina. Bizarrely it is said that he already prepared for a future embalming while Evita was alive. For instance, he treated burnt patches on her skin caused by the radiation treatments for her illness with oils. The actual mummification, however, commenced only immediately after the demise of Eva Perón with the injection of a preserving fluid via the main artery. By this means her body could survive the lying in state in the ventilated coffin without harm.

Subsequently Ara completed his work in a well-equipped laboratory within the palatial Union Hall. Hereby he injected a formalin solution into the veins of the dead woman and rinsed the body with formalin and zinc chloride. In contrast to Lenin the internal organs remained and were wrapped with strings of paraffin. Ara used further chemicals, such as borate, carbolic acid and mercury, and finally sealed the body with a layer of wax. The result of the embalming was impressive and Evita could be admired laid out on a white silk cloth in a chapel close to the laboratory.

The plan to erect a palatial mausoleum in the heart of the capital for the immortal Evita was abruptly brought to nought as a result of the putsch by Perón's adversaries in 1955. As she still possessed enormous popularity, the new regime decided to bury her mummified body in a secret location. Under the direction of Lieutenant-Colonel Carlos Eugenio Moori Koenig she was finally flown to Milan after accommodation in several hiding places. There she was interred under the name María Maggi de Magistris, probably with the collusion of the Vatican.

Evita's supporters did not stop looking for the mortal remains of their idol and in 1971 they succeeded in locating her final resting place in Milan. Thereupon the corpse was exhumed and brought to Juan Perón, now living in exile in Milan, who seemed unenthusiastic about this situation.

The consulted embalmer Pedro Ara confirmed the identity and integrity of the mummy, but concealed or ignored the heavy damage to face and body reported by Eva's sister. The embalmed corpse remained in Milan for the timebeing and was only brought back to Argentina after Juan Perón's death in 1974 at the behest of his third wife Isabella. There the mummy was immediately restored by Domingo Tellechea and kept in the residence until a further putsch two years later. Now Evita could finally be put to rest by her sisters in the family tomb of the Duartes in the Recoleta cemetery in Buenos Aires. The tomb has become a popular tourist attraction and today numerous people make the pilgrimage to the unforgettable Eva Perón to pray and to lay flowers, especially on Mother's Day.

Mummies from Egypt
Most people associate the term mummies with the elaborately mummified bodies of the famous rulers and nobility of ancient Egypt. After all, these have fascinated mankind for many hundreds of years, and also the word 'mummy' was derived from the Arabic mumia, meaning something like pitch or bitumen. This in turn was adopted from Persian where it originally described bee's wax. The interest in Egyptian mummies in Europe goes back to the thirteenth to sixteenth centuries, when a remedy of chopped or pulverised Egyptian mummy material labelled as Mumia or Mumia vera aegyptiaca gained increasing currency and importance. The curative effect of the remedy, which was still used until the 1920s, is extremely controversial. It has been rather ascribed to the sphere of magic and sorcery.

The scientific study with preserved corpses dates back to the work of Thomas Joseph Pettigrew, who in the mid nineteenth century for the first time described and documented in detail the unwrapping of an Egyptian mummy. Since then mummies from Egypt are a popular subject of study, and numerous scientific publications continue to address this topic. In the course of this interest the form of examination changed from at first purely descriptive observations to more and more complex analyses with the aid of various medical and scientific methods. Radiological techniques, and computer-based tomography in particular, have shown themselves to be suitable methodologies since they allow a destruction-free examination of mummies – an important aspect, if we consider the great significance of integrity and preservation ascribed to the mummy as a cultural asset today. For diverse examinations, as for example the analysis of DNA or isotopes, the taking of samples is unavoidable, but nowadays very small amounts are sufficient, whereby intensive and far-sighted planning is extremely important.

The beginnings of mummification in ancient Egypt date back to the so-called predynastic period, the epoch before the formation of the dynasties, in which the Egyptian kingdom was unified. Mummies from this period still originate from a natural mummification process favoured by the burial of the dead in dry desert sand. Yet there is already early evidence from some sites, as for example Saqqara and Abydos, that linen bandages soaked in resin were used for the preservation of the deceased.

The earliest mummies preserved by natural means date to about 3,500 BC, for instance the mummy with the nickname Ginger in the British Museum in London. Early signs of attempts of artificial mummification were found in the tomb complex of Djer, a 1st Dynasty king ruling in the thirty-first century BC. Here the British archaeologist Flinders Petrie, during his excavations at Abydos, found a forearm wrapped in bandages and decorated with rich jewellery. It could not be clarified until now whether this arm belonged to the king, his wife or another occupant of the tomb. During the Old Kingdom (c.2,700-2,200 BC) a more and more elaborate mummification practice developed.

There is evidence already from the 4th Dynasty that internal organs

Apothecary jar with 'mumia'.

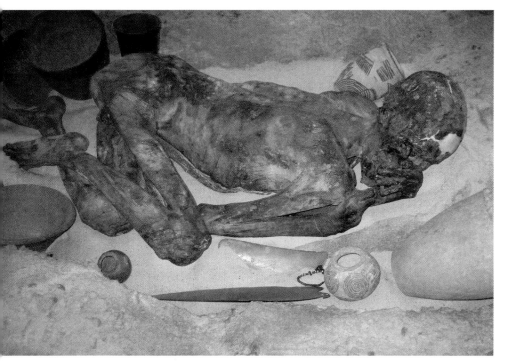

Predynastic mummy from Gebelein ('Ginger'), British Museum London.

were removed by way of an incision into the abdomen in order to facilitate the dehydration of the body. The removed organs were wrapped in linen bandages soaked with resin and some were placed in containers, canopic jars, or put into specific areas of the tomb. After the end of the Old Kingdom the bodies were increasingly wrapped in large amounts of linen bandages, even in simpler interments. In addition, a mummy mask fashioned from cartonnage became common, and the mummies were placed in coffins, sometimes richly decorated.

In the mummification itself large amounts of natron were used for the efficient dehydration of the body and the organs removed through an abdominal incision, though the brain was still infrequently removed. The empty cavity was subsequently stuffed with linen bandages, sawdust or Nile silt. The organs were interred together with the body in canopic jars.

During the New Kingdom (c.1,550-1,070 BC) mummification reached its pinnacle in ancient Egypt. The elaborate procedure encompassed the removal of the organs, including the brain through

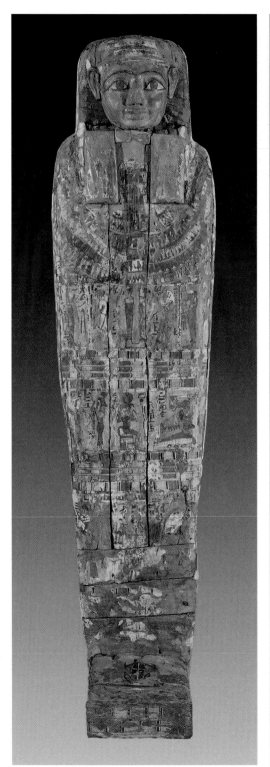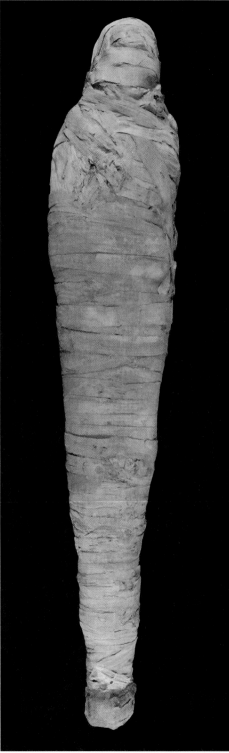

Mummy of Ankhpakhered. Left: Coffin. Right: Completely wrapped mummy.

the nose, the dehydration with natron, the use of different oils, resins, bitumen, wax, herbs and aromatics, the external and internal placement of amulets, and finally the wrapping in several layers of linen bandages. The heart usually remained inside the body, as it was seen as the seat of the soul, whereas some organs were placed into canopic jars, the lids of which were decorated with the heads of the four sons of the Egyptian god Horus.

In the New Kingdom anthropoid coffins were increasingly used. Sarcophagi of stone were initially reserved for kings, but were later used for the burial of private persons such as high officials. In the Late Period of the Egyptian empire the use of bitumen in the mummification process increased, which was partly poured into and over the bodies. The internal organs were often put back into the body, and on the whole a great variability is shown in the execution of the procedure.

During the Greco-Roman period a renaissance of mummification took place, characterised by a very complex and intricate wrapping of the bandages. Furthermore, so-called mummy portraits appear at this time, especially in the necropoleis of the Fayum, an oasis-like region south-west of Cairo, which are portraits of the deceased individuals on wooden tablets or directly on the mummy linen.

Male mummy portrait from the Fayum.

Tutankhamen, the Golden King

Probably the best-known pharaoh of Egyptian history is the young Tutankhamen. Hardly any other king fascinates people in the same manner and the material legacy from his tomb in the Valley of the Kings is simply the embodiment of a past civilisation. The numerous golden treasures, among them the famous golden mask shown in almost every report on ancient Egypt, let us sense the splendour,

101

*Howard Carter examines
Tutankhamen's coffin.*

wealth and power of the previous rulers of Egypt. No great deeds, such
as victorious battles or impressive edifices, have made Tutankhamen
so famous, but rather the simple discovery of his untouched tomb, long
hidden from tomb robbers and archaeologists alike.

It was not until 1922 that the British explorer Howard Carter
discovered the entrance to the tomb complex on the west bank of the
Nile near Thebes, modern-day Luxor. The relatively small-scale burial
site under its modern label KV62 contained an unbelievable wealth of
funerary objects made from vast amounts of gold, precious stones and
other most exclusive materials, which were to equip the king for
eternal life. Behind a bricked-up wall the actual burial chamber was
found, which contained four shrines and four sarcophagi in total, all
nested into each other. The innermost coffin was of pure gold and held

the richly decorated mummified remains of Tutankhamen, who was wrapped in thick bandages and whose head and shoulders were covered with the radiant golden mask.

The coffins and also the golden mask were evidently doused with large amounts of a substance containing bitumen during the funerary ritual. In the course of time the resin-like material hardened and could later only be removed with great difficulty by Howard Carter's assistants. The golden mask was so firmly fused with the mummy that considerable damage was done during its removal. Tutankhamen's mummy is by far not as well-preserved as those of other pharaohs of the same dynasty. Rather atypical for this period large amounts of bitumen were used in his mummification, and in general the procedure seems to have been carried out less carefully and possibly in great haste. That the body of the king was rather simply or hastily prepared in comparison to the very elaborate and valuable funerary equipment

Tutankhamen's mummy.

might be explained by the possibly sudden death of the king. It is also conceivable that the young pharaoh died far away from his residence and that his corpse already showed signs of advanced decomposition on his return, which made a quick treatment necessary. However, no historical records exist for this theory and hence we can only speculate about the reasons.

Tutankhamen died young, at the age of 18 to 20. He was a king of the 18th Dynasty of ancient Egypt, which ruled over the country from 1550 to 1295 BC and forms the epoch of the so-called New Kingdom together with the 19th and 20th Dynasties (1550 to 1070 BC). He became pharaoh around 9 years of age, and his reign lasted a mere nine years further, from 1332 BC till his death in 1323 BC. Despite the rich funerary equipment little was known about the family background of Tutankhamen or about the cause that snatched the young king so early from life. It was one of the great riddles of Egyptian history who his parents were and how exactly the royal family tree was composed. His predecessor as pharaoh Akhenaten, also known as the heretic king, and the enigmatic Smenkhkare offered themselves as likely paternal candidates. His mother might have been Akhenaten's first wife, the beautiful Nefertiti, but also his second wife Kiya.

Up to that point no securely ascribed mummy existed for any of these persons, which made the identification of Tutankhamen's parentage even more difficult. This situation was the starting point of a large-scale project by the Institute of the Mummies and the Iceman in collaboration with the University of Tübingen and the National Research Centre in Cairo, under the direction of the Egyptian Supreme Council of Antiquities with its then director Zahi Hawass. Together we attempted to investigate the ancestry and family background of the golden pharaoh and obtain more detailed information on possible illnesses and the cause of death, as far as this is possible. To this end, eleven mummies ascribed to the 18th Dynasty were available in total. Some were securely identified on historical grounds, whereas others were considered potential royal mummies merely on the basis of the find context or other evidence. Among the latter is an almost completely skeletonised mummy found in the tomb KV55 and ascribed to Akhenaten or Smenkhkare. In addition, there were the well-preserved mummified remains of two female

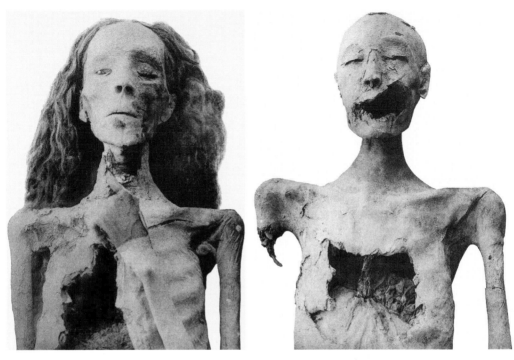

Younger and older woman from tomb KV35 in the Valley of the Kings.

individuals coming from tomb KV35 and conveniently called Younger Lady and Elder Lady due to their different ages. On the basis of the manner of mummification both ladies fit well into the 18th Dynasty, and some Egyptologists believed they could identify the younger woman as Nefertiti or Kiya, both wives of Akhenaten, and the elder woman likewise as Nefertiti or as Queen Tiy, the wife of the long-reigning pharaoh Amenhotep III. Clear historical evidence, however, could not be provided. Furthermore, the mummies of two foetuses came from the tomb of Tutankhamen, both of which apparently died in the womb, and for both of which it was not evident if they were descendants of the king or interred with him for other reasons.

Two further, relatively badly preserved mummies from the tomb KV21 in the Valley of the Kings were included in the project, since these were potential candidates for Ankhesenamun, the young royal wife of Tutankhamen. Besides Tutankhamen's mummy those of his

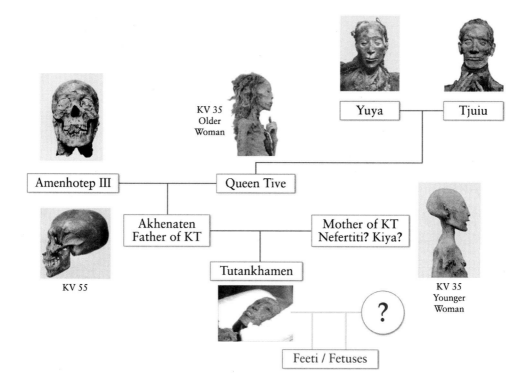

Genealogy of Tutankhamen's royal family.

maternal great-grandparents, Yuya and Tuya, and that of Amenhotep III count among the securely identified mummies of ancient Egypt.

The eleven mummies underwent detailed anthropological, radiological and molecular biological examinations, in order to define the exact age of the individuals, to receive evidence for possible diseases, and to clarify the familial relationships of the royal family of the 18th Dynasty. For the genetic analyses of the familial relationships, several samples in form of small bone punches from the interior of the large long bones (femur, tibia and humerus) were taken from all mummies under sterile conditions. The radiological examinations could be carried out with a mobile CT scanner on hand at the Egyptian Museum in Cairo.

For the genetic analyses the bone samples were further processed in a laboratory specifically established for this purpose in a side wing of the museum. There the existing genetic material of the royal mummies was extracted in a complex procedure and so the genetic fingerprints of the separate individuals were produced. With the aid of statistical methods the results were evaluated, and from this a genetic family tree of the royal family could be reconstructed.

Hereby, the skeletal mummy from tomb KV55 could be identified as Tutankhamen's father on the one hand, and on the other the younger woman from KV35 as his mother. Furthermore the elder woman was identified with great certainty as the daughter of Yuya and Tuya and thus Queen Tiy. Interestingly it was revealed that both the younger woman and the skeleton from KV 55 were children from her union with Amenhotep III, and hence Tutankhamen was identified as the offspring of a sibling marriage.

The examinations of the two foetuses from Tutankhamen's tomb did not yield complete genetic fingerprints, but resulted in evidence that both stillbirths might be indeed direct descendants of the young king. Historical records are also necessary, in addition to the genetic evidence, to identify Tutankhamen's parents for certain. In the case of his father, new archaeological evidence might be presented by the Egyptian team indicating that the coffin, in which the mummified corpse was found, belonged to Akhenaten. Thin gold plating originally attached to the coffin and depicting the solar god Aten supports this fact. Earlier anatomical examinations on the skeleton from KV55 resulted in an age of only 25, so it was impossible to ascribe it to Akhenaten. The radiological age determination on the basis of the computer-based tomographic images indicated, however, a much higher age and therefore the identification of KV55 with Akhenaten can be considered as very likely on this basis. Yet as long as no further information can be provided on the life and whereabouts of the mysterious Smenkhkare, he cannot be excluded entirely as the potential father of Tutankhamen.

During earlier radiological examinations of the mummy of Tutankhamen the age at death could be determined as 19 to 20, but no secure insights into the cause of death could be gained. Occasionally various murder scenarios were even conceived on the basis of misinterpretation of X-ray images, which did not withstand critical scientific verification. On the other hand the unhealed fracture in the area of the left knee, detected during a previous examination, was correctly diagnosed. As no signs of a healing process can be observed here, the injury must have occurred shortly before death and might thus be connected to the demise of the young king. Yet there is no evidence for the assumption that blood poisoning might have occurred as a consequence of the injury or that the fracture was possibly caused by a fall from a chariot, and so this has to be considered as speculation.

The renewed evaluation of the CT images yielded new insights into the physical condition of the golden pharaoh. Clear indications of an acute inflammatory osteo-necrosis were found in his left foot, the Freiberg-Köhler syndrome, besides a slight club foot. The disease, typically occurring in adolescents and associated in its acute form with swelling of the forefoot and severe pain, led with great certainty to a significant restriction of the young king's mobility. Therefore it can be assumed that the scenes depicting Tutankhamen supported by a walking stick indeed reflect the actual facts. The assumption that Tutankhamen required a walking aid probably until his death is underpinned by Howard Carter's find of 130 staffs in the former's tomb, partly complete, partly fragmented.

Evidence for the possible cause of death of the golden pharaoh was provided by further molecular biological studies in the context of our project, during which we examined genetic material for possible infectious diseases. For this molecular tests for different pathogens were carried out. During the diagnostic procedures the malaria pathogen Plasmodium falciparum was detected in Tutankhamen, but also in the mummies of Yuya and Tuya. This micro-organism causes the form of malaria that is, in most cases, associated with marked anaemia and neurological complications and can take a severe course.

The detection of malaria pathogens in Tutankhamen does not allow for direct conclusions on the cause of death. The findings show that the short-lived king suffered from several illnesses that must have impaired him considerably, and which probably weakened his immune system. An injury, such as a simple fall, possibly caused by an existing walking disability or the infection with malaria might finally have led to Tutankhamen's demise. In order to answer the question to what extent the attested sibling marriage of Tutankhamen's parents and possibly further cases within the royal family had an unfavourable

Walk in the garden of Amarna. The relief shows Tutankhamen supported by a walking stick, Egyptian Museum Berlin.

effect on the genome of the young pharaoh and his relatives, further detailed examinations are necessary.

Ramses III and the Harem's Conspiracy

Ramses III was an Egyptian king of the New Kingdom and son and successor of Pharaoh Sethnakht, the founder of the 20th Dynasty. He was born around 1221 BC, ascended to the throne in 1188 BC and died on 7 April 1156 BC, according to historical sources. The end of Ramses III's life was for many years the cause of extensive discussions among Egyptologists. In a number of documents, among which the Turin juridical papyrus is the most important, it is described how members of his harem made an attempt on Ramses' life in the course of a palace revolt. According to the historical sources the *coup d'etat* failed, but they shed no light on whether the assassination was also

Temple of Ramses III in the temple complex of Karnak.

unsuccessful. The Turin juridical papyrus reports on four different trials and lists the imposed punishments for those involved in the conspiracy.

Queen Tiy, a secondary wife of Ramses III, and her son Prince Pentawer were identified as the leaders of the revolt. The punishments ranged from cutting off noses and ears to execution. Some high officials received the order to commit suicide. In all records Ramses III is named as the great god, and other phrases also speak for the fact that the king was already dead at the time of the trials. On the other hand the pharaoh officiated as prosecutor and the court received its orders directly from him. This might be interpreted as meaning that Ramses III was still alive at the beginning of the trials and thus initially survived the assassination attempt. Other scholars interpret this as the divine power of the king who controls the fate of his people even after death.

Due to the ambiguous textual sources and lack of clues for the cause of death from previous examinations of the royal mummy, various theories on the outcome of the harem's conspiracy were developed. Either the attempt on Ramses III failed completely, or it was successful and led directly to his death, or the pharaoh was badly injured and later died of his injuries. Nothing is known of the fate of Queen Tiy, while it is assumed of her son Pentawer that he had to commit suicide. The mummy of the prince could not be identified for a long time, but some scholars suspected that the mummy known as Unknown Man E might be the royal son. This was found together with those of Ramses III and other royal mummies in the Deir el-Bahari cachette, a tomb complex probably dating to the 22nd Dynasty, which served as a depot for numerous royal mummies to protect them from tomb robbers.

In order to figure out the real outcome of the harem's conspiracy another project was started by the Institute for Mummies and the Iceman and the same German-Egyptian team, which had already carried out the Tutankhamen study. This project should answer the question of Ramses III's fate and of the identity of the mummy Unknown Man E with radiological, forensic and molecular biological methods. For this purpose both mummies were examined in a CT scanner and bone samples were taken and underwent a genetic analysis.

111

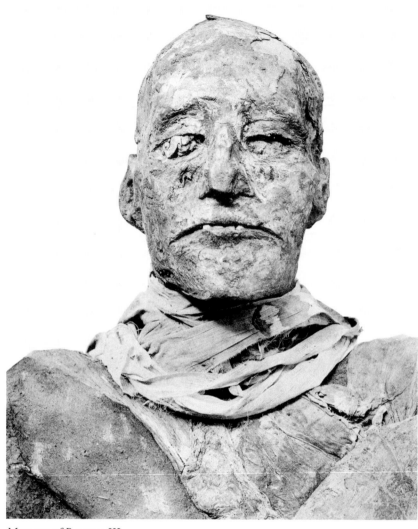

Mummy of Ramses III.

To our great surprise the CT images showed a deep gaping wound in the area of Ramses' neck. The injury, which was very likely caused by a sharp-edged object, probably a knife or sword, is roughly 70mm wide and stretches from the left to the right side of the throat. It reaches the cervical vertebrae, and the complete soft tissue of the frontal neck was injured. The windpipe was severed, and the ends of the incision are clearly separated from each other. In addition to the cut through the throat, the gullet and the large blood vessels were injured too.

The extent and the severity of the injury allow only one conclusion: Ramses was severely injured by a cut across the throat and must have died immediately as a consequence. The find of an amulet in the form of an eye of Horus inside the wound provided evidence that the cut was not made post-mortem, for example in the process of mummification. Based on three-dimensional reconstructions of the CT images the object could be virtually replicated and is roughly 15mm in size. The eye of Horus represents a protective symbol and was used by the ancient Egyptian priests as a sign for restitution or healing. Obviously these tried to symbolically heal the wound for the afterlife through the insertion of such an amulet during the mummification of the king.

Therefore it could be proven with high certainty that Ramses III indeed fell victim to an assassination in the course of the harem's conspiracy and did not survive. The fatal neck injury remained hidden during earlier examinations, as a broad collar of bandages covered this area, and only the radiological examination was able to provide clarification. It was further shown that the king, aged over 60 at death, suffered from severe arteriosclerosis including the coronary vessels and thus possessed a significantly heightened risk of heart attack. Inside his body additional amulets were found, showing the four sons of Horus.

Mummy of Unknown Man E.

The examinations of the unknown male revealed that this man was mummified in a manner entirely atypical for that period. There are no signs at all on his body of incisions for the removal of the internal organs or the brain. The mummy's skin shows a slight reddish tinge, and it emits an unpleasant, pungent smell. The widely gaping mouth has earned him the nickname 'screaming mummy' and has fanned discussions about a possible burial whilst he was still alive. However, this phenomenon can be observed very frequently on natural mummies, where the dehydration can lead to such a distortion of the facial features. Yet this has, as a rule, nothing to do with the manner of interment and certainly does not portray an expression of horror in the deceased individual.

Nevertheless the unknown man was evidently buried in a very unusual manner. He was undressed and not wrapped in mummy bandages but merely covered with a goatskin. Furthermore we could determine during the forensic inspection that the genitals were missing and conspicuous folds of skin had formed around the neck. These conveyed the impression that possibly a rope had been wound around the neck. On the radiological image the mummy in addition displayed a bloated upper torso as well as signs of gas formation in the abdominal region due to degradation, These features speak for the fact that the unknown man did not die a natural death, but was possibly strangled or hanged.

Due to the lack of further evidence this cannot be verified for certain. Nonetheless it is confirmed that he did not undergo regular mummification and hence probably had not received an honourable burial. The genetic examination should clarify whether he might be the royal son Pentawer who was found guilty by the judges as co-conspirator of the palace revolt and probably sentenced to suicide. A comparison of the genetic fingerprints indeed revealed a 50 percent match of the used markers between Ramses III and Unknown Man E. In addition a complete concordance was found in the genetic signature of the Y chromosome, i.e. the male sex chromosome. Therefore a relationship along the paternal line between the two individuals could be established and based on the similarities in the genetic fingerprints concluded that the unknown man was a son of Ramses III.

Unfortunately no mummy of the mother, Queen Tiy, is preserved, hence the test cannot provide 100 percent certainty that the unusual mummy is Prince Pentawer. Yet if we view the unusual manner of mummification, the clues for a violent death – possibly suicide by hanging – and the genetic proximity to Ramses III together, the identification of Unknown Man E as Pentawer seems quite plausible. Even if scientific doubts of the mummy's identity remain, this research project could solve the great riddle of the outcome of the harem's conspiracy, and an important chapter in the history of ancient Egypt could be closed.

The great pharaoh Ramses III fell victim of an insidious revolt, during which his throat was cut in a brutal manner. The historical sources reveal that the uprising failed and the conspirators received their punishment, among them evidently also the perceived successor to the throne, Prince Pentawer.

Mummies from Asia

As all other continents, Asia also offers numerous mummies from various periods. These range from the roughly 4,000-year-old mummies of the Central Asian Tarim basin to the burials of the Scythian Pazyryk culture dating approximately 500 BC, the moist corpses of the Chinese Han period (206 BC to 220 AD), the Korean and Japanese mummies of the last 600 to 700, years all the way to the modern embalmed bodies of Ho Chi Min and Mao Zedong, founder of the People's Republic of China. Equally as diverse as the date and

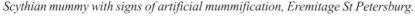

Scythian mummy with signs of artificial mummification, Eremitage St Petersburg.

geographic distribution of the mummies are the mummification techniques and the climatic conditions as well as the specific coffin environments that have led to the preservation of the bodies.

The mummies of the Pazyryk culture in modern Mongolia show clear indications of artificial mummification. It was established, for example, for the Altai Lady, a Scythian princess discovered on the Ukok plateau in the Altai mountains, that she underwent an elaborate procedure after her death. Initially the internal organs were removed via an incision in the upper body, subsequently the abdomen was filled with a mixture of sand, wool and herbs, and the chest stuffed with dry peat. The brain was removed and the empty skull padded with horse hair. In addition traces of wax, clay and mercury were found on the skin of the mummy, which were applied for the purpose of preservation, probably also to enable the exhibition of the corpse for a certain period, as it is known from historical sources that Scythian rulers travelled one last time through their kingdom after their death.

This was only possible in a mummified state. The interment itself took place in the type of burial mound typical for the culture, the kurgans. The subterranean wooden constructions were covered with gravel and grass roots, through which melted water seeped during the summer, turning the ensemble into an ice lens in the winter. These circumstances improved the conditions for preservation significantly and led to the extraordinarily good preservation of the organic grave goods, such as carpets, clothing and furs.

In the year after the discovery of the ice princess and not far from that place, the mummy of a Scythian warrior was found, who was buried together with his horse. Like the Altai Lady the man displayed tattoos in the form of animal motifs on his upper body, and he had reddish blond hair.

In recent years the German archaeologist Hermann Parzinger managed to track down further mummies of the Pazyryk culture, among them the preserved body of a 30- to 40-year-old warrior with blond hair, buried with two horses and a wealth of burial goods, including, for example, the composite bow often mentioned in ancient Greek literature.

In contrast to the artificially mummified bodies of the Scythian warriors, in China numerous examples of a natural mummification process are found, which is either caused by specific climatic conditions or a special chemical composition of the coffin interior. In Xingjiang in the far west of China high temperatures prevail for most of the time and extreme aridity exists. Especially in the basin of Turfan temperatures of 70 to 80° C can be reached during summer. The annual rainfall is below 17mm, and the ground water level is found at a depth of more than 20m.

These exceedingly dry and hot climatic conditions led to the fact that those buried in numerous graves of the Tarim basin near Lake Lop Nor were mummified by natural means. The burial complexes, often only a few metres below ground, date predominantly to a period between the eighth century BC and tenth century AD. Some cemeteries date back to roughly 1800 BC. Among them is the necropolis of Käwirgul, situated approximately 70km west of the dried up Lake

Mummy from the Tarim basin, the 'beauty of Lulan'.

117

Lop Nor besides the lower course of the River Konqi, on top of a small dune. Here archaeologists found forty-two graves of men, women and children lying extended on their backs in an east-west orientation. The extreme aridity and the high salt content of the soil resulted in an excellent preservation of the interred bodies. Among them were found completely mummified corpses, for instance the beauty of Lulan, who can be admired today in a museum in Urumqi. She displays, like the other early interments of the Tarim basin, a rather European (Caucasian) physiognomy, an impression evoked by the narrow face with a long, pointed nose and the reddish brown hair.

Other mummies from this region equally show signs of European origin, as for example the tall red-haired Cherchen Man (1000 BC), the Hami mummy – an equally red-haired woman from Qizilhoqa – or the witches of Subeshi, who wore tall black conical felt hats and typical European clothing.

In contrast, at the eastern margin of the Tarim basin twenty-nine mummies were found in the necropolis of Yanbulag, who showed predominantly Asian or Mongolian features. The tombs date to a period from 1100 to 500 BC, and furthermore contained eight mummies more closely resembling European types from other sites.

The mainly European physiognomy and dress of the mummies from the Tarim basin have led to heated discussions about the origin of past inhabitants and the settlement of the modern Xinjiang region. Speculations on European settlement and a strong western influence on Chinese culture were further enhanced by the location of sites along the Silk Road. According to recent knowledge based on both archaeological and genetic examinations of the mummies, however, the early population of the Tarim basin shows both western and eastern Eurasian influences. Therefore it is now no longer assumed that settlers from Europe immigrated there, but rather population groups who previously had lived in the region of the Altai mountains, i.e. in the frontier region between modern Russia, Kazakhstan and Mongolia. In addition Mongolian tribes settled along the eastern margin of the Tarim basin and, furthermore, settlement of the region also took place from the direction of the western steppe. In the course of time the different ethnic groups began to interact and amalgamate.

118

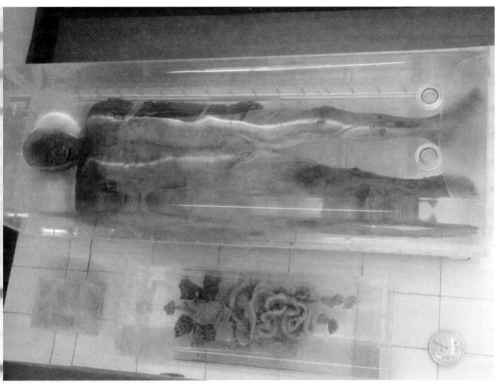

Chinese mummy from Jinghzou, Han Dynasty, Jingzhou Museum.

In the heartland of China the conceptions about the meaning of death and the treatment of the departed were subject to certain change. In principle a high regard of the dead existed, who as ancestors claimed special veneration. Furthermore, the desire of immortality and eternal time grew in the course of time. Especially during the Han period (206 BC to 220 AD) alchemy was conducted with great enthusiasm, essentially with the aim to produce an immortality pill. In addition it was attempted to conquer death by the ingestion of vermilion water or mercury, the eating of blossoms, mushrooms, pine nuts and fruit as well as exercises in fasting and breathing or special sexual practices. Naturally these efforts were not crowned with success.

The deceased individuals were buried according to Confucian funerary rites. Hereby several months could pass between the time of death until the actual interment, depending on the status of the dead. This made it necessary to preserve the corpses at least for a limited period of time. Although no mummification in the true sense, for example by organ removal, was carried out, the deceased persons were initially washed and subsequently immersed into an alcoholic bath, consisting mainly of cereal wine with aromatic supplements. The corpse was finally wrapped in several layers of silk garments and blankets and laid out on a bier, under which a basin with ice was placed for cooling purposes. During the funeral different aromatic substances and incense materials were often added, so for example rue, magnolia buds, cinnamon bark and sandalwood.

The putrefaction-repelling nature of mercury was known in China for a long time and it was therefore also ingested as a purported means to prolong life. In addition it was used in the treatment of vermicular diseases. In contrast it was probably less well-known that mercury is highly toxic and that its ingestion results in severe damage to the liver and kidneys. Therefore it can be presumed that the intake of mercury and mercury compounds had the opposite effect, yet which proved to be advantageous for mummification. After all, we know from experience with mercury poisonings that the decomposition process of the victims is often considerably hampered. Besides mercury ingested during life archaeological evidence was found that mercury compounds were directly placed into coffins too, which in some cases were found at the bottom of the coffin together with a layer of charcoal.

A further cause for the mummification of corpses was the use of several thick-walled, nested wooden coffins, which created an environment very low in oxygen and thus could slow down the decomposition process or even halt it altogether. For this some finds were made from the Ming dynasty (1368 to 1644 AD). Furthermore the natural mummification process was supported by the construction of very deep tomb shafts penetrating up to 20m into the ground, and by the filling of the burial chamber with different materials, such as, for instance, shell limestone, charcoal and kaolin. A similar type of burial in the tombs found in South Korea also resulted in the mummification of those interred.

A particularly unusual form of natural-intentional mummification is found in Japan. There relatively disadvantageous natural conditions for a permanent preservation of deceased individuals as mummies prevail due to the warm and humid climate. Nonetheless, around twenty Japanese mummies could be examined and described. The deceased persons are in the majority clergy, but four of them come from the ruling family of Fujiwara in northern Honshu. Especially impressive, however, are the self-mummifications of Buddhist monks belonging predominantly to the Japanese Shingon sect. This mummification practice, described as Sokushinbutsu, was seen in the teachings of Shingon-shū as a possibility to pass over into Nirvana by the extreme neglect of the body in favour of the spirit. The actual process of mummification took place in several steps, for which the decision was made deliberately by each person.

In the first step over a period of 1,000 days initially the diet was strictly reduced, for which the usual foodstuffs were renounced entirely and replaced by tree bark, wild herbs and pine tree roots. At the end of this diet the monk commenced with the drinking of a toxic tea from the resin of the Urushi tree, which triggers vomiting and strong sweating and promotes the dehydration of the body. At the end of this process he was then locked in a ventilated stone chamber or buried therein, if he had already died. After another 1,000 days the mummification was completed, where required the mummy was dried with the aid of smoke or heat and subsequently dressed in a monk's robe.

At the end of the nineteenth century self-mummification was prohibited in Japan. In 1903 the last monk died during the performance of this ritual. Many of the monks' mummies are today in a relatively bad state of preservation and therefore need special attention.

Lady Dai, a mummy from the Han Dynasty in China
A particularly remarkable mummy was found at the beginning of the 1970s in Mawangdui near Changsha in the Hunan province. In a double tumulus three tombs of the ruling family of Dai were found, which date to the Western Han period (206 BC to 24 AD). The tombs belonged to Li Chang, First Marquis of Dai and chancellor of the kingdom of Changsha, his wife Xin Zhui and an approximately 30-year-old man, probably their son. The tomb of the Marquis of Dai,

who died in 186 BC, was looted repeatedly by tomb robbers and as a consequence badly damaged. A mummy of the chancellor is not preserved.

The other two tombs withstood the test of time undisturbed, but only in the tomb of the Marquise of Dai was a mummified corpse found, while the tomb of the presumed son only contained a skeleton.

Excavation at the tomb complex of the ruling family of Dai.

The state of preservation of the lady was all the more spectacular, so that she is sometimes considered the best preserved mummy in the world. She was found inside four nested lacquered coffins. The innermost coffin was completely filled with items of clothing and blankets in addition to a yellow-brown liquid in which the corpse was half-immersed. The tomb of the lady contained, among other items, a completely preserved cosmetic kit, lacquered bowls for drinking wine and finely woven silk garments, which were decorated with impressive paintings. Furthermore a silken funeral banner was found on top of Lady Dai's coffin, with a painting portraying the Chinese conception of the cosmos and afterlife at the time of the Western Han period.

In addition tomb number three yielded maps painted on silk, the earliest finds of this kind in China.

The mummified corpse of the lady was initially kept in a 4-5 percent formaldehyde solution after its recovery and later underwent a thorough examination. The good state of preservation of the body still showing a certain elasticity permitted even the performance of an autopsy. The Princess of Dai died at the approximate age of 50. The mummy showed a physical height of 154cm and weighed 34.3kg at the inspection. The relatively heavy weight for a mummified corpse is explained by the relatively high content of moisture in the body. This is probably related to the fluid inside the coffin. Its analysis revealed that it was very acidic with a pH-value of 5.18. Additionally, it contained a small portion of mercury and high concentrations of phosphor, magnesium and natrium. Its origin and the exact procedure of the mummification are still unexplained today.

In the opinion of the Chinese researchers this fluid had formed only after the interment and contributed to the preservation of the princess. Yet it is possible that the mercury-rich liquid was added deliberately during the burial because of the already known putrefaction-repelling characteristics of the heavy metal. In any case it can be assumed that the low pH-value, the high salt content and the mercury contributed significantly to the mummification. The process was certainly supported by the virtually airtight closure of the nested coffins, further enhanced by the construction of the burial chamber. The latter was constructed at the depth of 20m, filled with 60 tons of coal and, in addition, sealed with a thick layer of loam.

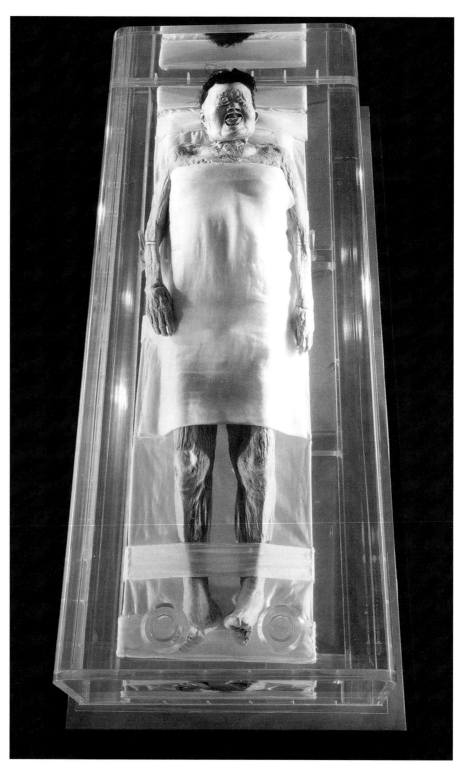

Mummy of Lady Dai, Provincial Museum of Hunan.

Especially unusual is the state of preservation of the skin, which was still relatively soft and pliable, a fact later also shown for the internal organs. The surface of the skin, however, was uneven and showed several indications of hypodermic formation of grave wax. Most of the joints were still slightly moveable. Certain signs of the process of putrefaction are found, as for example the sunken eyes and a slightly protruding tongue, which had evidently been halted at some point.

The autopsy showed that the brain was still well-preserved and had shrunken to roughly half its original size. The hair on the head was still entirely intact. Cause of death was a myocardial infarction of the heart, presumably triggered by a bilious attack. The princess already suffered from a severe calcification of the left coronary artery at that time, which had reduced the volume of the artery by 25 to 50 percent. Her last meal consisted of a musk melon, the seeds of which were found in great numbers in the stomach and gullet. The pathological findings revealed further clues for general arteriosclerosis, the occurrence of gall stones, nodular calcifications in the lung, a slipped disc in the area of the lumbar column, and old, healed fractures of the right lower arm

Hand-painted silk cloth from Lady Dai's tomb.

bones. Furthermore, evidence was found in the liver and the intestinal walls for an infection with Schistosoma japonica, a cause for bilharzia, a vermicular disease that can lead to severe liver damage. On top of that, eggs of the parasites whipworm (Trichuris trichura) and threadworm (Enterobius vermicularis) could be attested.

Chemical analyses resulted in significantly heightened levels of lead in the bones and the wall of the aorta and in a value of mercury far above the usual levels in kidneys and liver. Concentrations of vermilion and lead in the area of the small intestine clearly show that the substances were already ingested during life.

The ingestion of heavy metal compounds was seen as a life-prolonging measure at that time. On the other hand, the severe infestation with worms and parasites of Lady Dai could have likewise been a reason for the intake of these compounds.

The mummy of Xin Zhui, Princess of Dai, is exhibited today in the provincial museum of Hunan, together with the impressive grave goods.

South Korean mummies, swathed in silk

Less well-known than the Chinese mummies and in particular Lady Dai, but not less fascinating, are the mummies from South Korea. These only gained increasing scientific interest in the last ten years, thanks to the efforts of the anatomist and mummy specialist Dong Hoon Shin of Seoul National University. Shin and his team have managed in recent years to scientifically examine some of the mummies little known before, and to find out interesting details on the manner of mummification, dietary habits and especially illnesses of the past inhabitants of South Korea.

Most Korean mummies date to the Joseon Dynasty lasting from 1392 to 1910 AD. As a rule, these come from graves belonging to the representatives of the ruling class, land owners, scholars or members of the royal court. In contrast to the ordinary population, higher ranking personalities received a special burial, for which the tomb was virtually sealed with a limestone and soil mixture. Inside the limestone barrier the wooden coffin or two nested coffins were found, which in turn contained the corpse thickly swathed in silken and cotton garments. This special form of burial led to the natural mummification of the corpses of high ranking personages.

This was very likely helped by the complete sealing of the wooden coffins by the limestone mantle and thus a mostly oxygen-free atmosphere, as well as the large amount of clothing and blankets that almost completely filled the interior of the coffin. In contrast to this, conventional interments consisted of simple coffins placed directly into the ground, leading to no mummification of the dead. Although

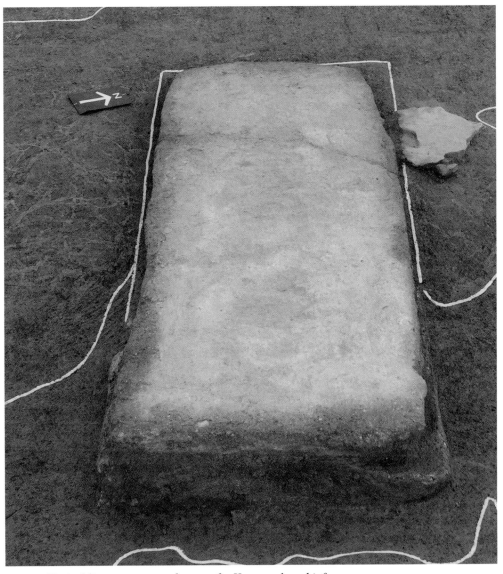

Typical limestone sarcophagus of a Korean clan chief.

these were buried in the same cemeteries, merely skeletons were found in the graves.

Interestingly, in some coffins of the South Korean mummies, similar to the Chinese mummies of the Han Dynasty, a rather moist environment existed, and some mummified corpses likewise showed a certain remaining moisture. Yet no larger amounts of fluid were found inside the coffins, as for example in the case of Lady Dai. Also, no evidence for the presence of mercury or other heavy metals came to light inside the coffins or in the internal organs of the mummies.

In recent years about ten of the mummies preserved in this manner underwent an intensive scientific study. The scientific possibilities depended very much on the respective descendants who in each case had to give their consent to the examinations. In previous times, therefore, many Korean mummies were reburied after a preliminary assessment and were not available for a thorough scientific analysis. For this reason Korean researchers attempt to increase the use of non-invasive or minimally invasive examination techniques, so for instance computer-based tomography or endoscopy, in order to avoid damage to the mummies, or to reduce it to a minimum. This general trend in modern mummy research represents a suitable measure to be able to return the mummies mostly intact to the descendants, and supports the endeavour to view mummies as important historical witnesses and also as cultural heritage, and to maintain their long-term preservation.

The studies of the South Korean mummy specialists provided many details on the mummies' state of preservation, for which frequently the entire internal organs and also the brain survived in excellent condition. Similar as in other mummies, here too the connective tissue and the collagen structures were for the most part very well-preserved, in addition to some cellular components, for example red blood cells, cartilage cells, and liver and muscle cells. The good retention of the digestive system, including the stomach contents, permitted the detection of numerous parasites within the mummies. Eggs and larvae of whipworms (Trichuris trichuria), roundworms (Ascaris lumbricoides), Chinese liver flukes (Clonorchis sinensis), threadworms (Strongyloides stercoralis, Trichostrongylus *spp*), lungworms (Paragonimus westermani) and distomae (Metagonimus yokogawai) could be identified, partly in great numbers. In some cases other illnesses could be identified too, and occasionally even the cause of death.

In 2007 the mummy of a man was found and uncovered in one of the typical tomb complexes sealed with limestone in the city of

The mummy of Gyenongsun.

Gangneung during the transfer of the ancestral remains of the local Choi clan. Thanks to the existing written records of the clan and the inscription on the tombstone, a personal profile of the deceased could be reconstructed. The founder of the clan, with the name Munhan, lived from 1320 to 1395 AD and was a son-in-law of the then king of the Goryeo dynasty (918 to 1392 AD). After the fall of the dynasty he moved with his family to the city of Gangneung. The mummified corpse from the tomb is a man called Gyeongsun, a descendant of Munhan in the eighth generation. His father, Unwoo, was, according to historical sources, a famous scholar and belonged to one of the most esteemed families of the kingdom.

Gyeongsun was born in 1561 and died in 1622 at the age of 61. His official title written on the tombstone was that of a deputy general of

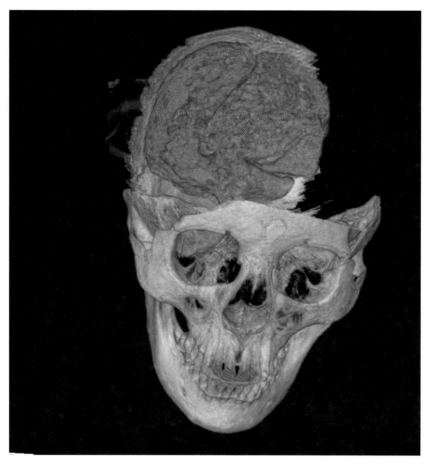

This CT image shows the excellent state of preservation of the brain.

the military command of the kingdom, probably rather a honorific title and hardly his actual position. The mummy was swathed in several layers of silken and cotton garments and showed an extraordinary state of preservation.

After the unwrapping of the head even individual hairs of the beard could be clearly discerned. During the medical examination in this case, eggs of the whipworm were found, but apart from that no signs of serious ailments were found. The still partially filled bowels indicated that the departed had still eaten regular food two days prior to his death. This leads to the assumption that death came quite suddenly and surprisingly. Clues to the cause of death were finally revealed in the CT scan of the mummy. Here a fresh, unhealed fracture of the mandible was revealed. Due to the lack of evidence of a healing process it has to be presumed that the general came by this injury immediately before his death and might have died as its consequence.

A unique example for the deep mourning caused by the death of a family member was found in the sepulchre of Eung Tae, who was accidentally discovered during construction works in the South Korean city of Andong. The man, who died in 1586, evidently left his wife behind, who gave free rein to her mourning in the form of love letters that she gave to her beloved husband for his final journey. The mummy was equipped with seventy-three pieces of clothing in total, which in part also came from his wife and their child. In addition shoes braided from woman's hair and further letters from relatives were found.

Mummy of Eung Tae swathed in numerous layers of garments.

An extract from the woman's letters describes very vividly her despair:

> *You always said, "Dear, let's live together until our hair turns grey and die on the same day. How could you pass away without me? Who should I and our little boy listen to and how should we live? How could you go ahead of me?*
>
> *...*
>
> *I just cannot live without you. I just want to go to you. Please take me to where you are. My feelings toward you I cannot forget in this world and my sorrow knows no limit. Where would I put my heart in now and how can I live with the child missing you?*

The mummy of Eung Tae was reburied on the same day of its excavation and thus it was not possible to examine the corpse in detail in order to find the cause of his demise. Yet the recovered grave goods give an immediate insight into the world of an early Korean family's emotions.

The Korean researchers achieved another remarkable find in collaboration with an Israeli research group. In liver samples of a male child's mummy – from the sixteenth century found in Yangju in Gyeonggi-do province – they could detect the Hepatitis B virus on molecular level. Hereby the entire genome sequence of the ancient virus could be reconstructed. A comparison with modern viral strains showed that it is a representative of the South Korean variety of Hepatitis B still widespread today. Furthermore, clear genetic differences to the modern strains were found, which are probably the result of environmental, immunological or medicinal influences. The common ancestor of the ancient and the modern strain of the virus must have occurred at least 3,000 years ago, but might even be 100,000 years old. With this the researchers not only succeeded in detecting probably the earliest form of Hepatitis B occurring in South Korea, but also in sequencing the first complete ancient viral genome.

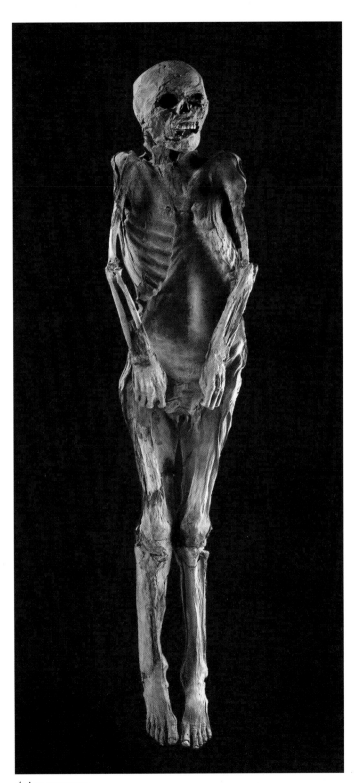

Asian mummy.

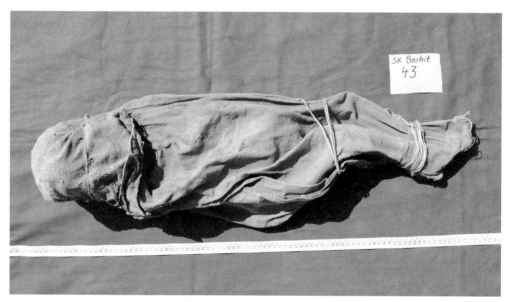

Child mummy from the Coptic monestary at Deir el-Bachit.

Selected Bibliography

Aufderheide, Arthur C. (2004) *The Scientific Study of Mummies.*
New York

Arriaza, Bernardo T. (1995) *Beyond Death: The Chinchorro Mummies of Ancient Chile.* Virginia

Barber, Elizabeth Wayland (1999) *The Mummies of Ürümchi.* New York – London

Brier, Bob (1998) *The Encyclopedia of Mummies.* New York

Buchele, Mark-Steffen (2006)
Der Ötzi – ein Medienereignis: Wirklichkeitsvermittlung im Spannungsfeld von Öffentlichkeitsarbeit und Journalismus. Eine Fallstudie zur jungneolithischen Mumie aus dem Gletscher vom Hauslabjoch. (Leipziger Forschungen zur Ur- und Frühgeschichtlichen Archäologie 6) 2nd edition, Leipzig

Cagnan, Paolo (2003) *Similaun e Juanita: Il mistero delle mummie rubato.* Milan

Capasso, Luigi (2000) *La mummia di Santa Rosa da Viterbo: antropologia, restauro e conservazione.* Bellante

Chamberlain, Andrew T. & Parker Pearson, Michael (2004)
Earthly Remains: The History and Science of Preserved Human Bodies. New York

Chioffi, Laura (1998) *Mummificazione ed imbalsamazione a Roma ded in altri luoghi del mondo romano (Opuscula epigraphica dell'Università degli Studi di Roma La Sapienza, Dipartmento di Scienze Storiche, Archeologiche, Antropologiche dell'Antichità 8).* Michigan

Cockburn, Thomas Aidan (ed) (2006) *Mummies, Disease and Ancient Cultures.* 2nd edition, Cambridge

Cowie, Susan D. & Johnson, Tom (2007) *The Mummy in Fact, Fiction and Film.* North Carolina

David, Ann Rosalie (ed) (2008) *Egyptian Mummies and Modern Science.* Cambridge

David, Ann Rosalie & Archbold, Rick (2009) *Conversations with Mummies: New Light on the Lives of Ancient Egyptians.* Madison Press Books

David, Ann Rosalie & Tapp, Eddie (eds) (1984) *Evidence Embalmed: Modern Medicine and the Mummies of Ancient Egypt.* Manchester

Deem, James M. (2008) *Bodies from the Ice. Melting Glaciers and the Recovery of the Past.* Boston

Drenkhahn, Rosemarie & Germer, Renate (eds) (1991) *Mumie und Computer. Ein multidisziplinäres Forschungsprojekt in Hannover. Katalog zur Sonderausstellung des Kestner-Museum Hannover vom 26. September 1991 bis 19. Januar 1992.* Hannover

Dunand, Françoise & Lichtenberg, Roger (2006) *Mummies and Death in Egypt.* Ithaca, New York

El Mahdy, Christine (2002) *Mummies, Myth and Magic in Ancient Egypt.* New York

Exhibition Mummies of the World 2010-2013, Los Angeles [in conjunction with the Exhibition "Mummies of the World", which tours selected venues in the United States from July 2010 through July 2013]

Fiałek, Elbieta (2001) *Mummy: results of interdisciplinary examination of the Egyptian mummy of Aset-iri-khet-es from the Archaeological Museum in Cracow [Thdeo Smolenski in memoriam].* Cracow

Fleckinger, Angelika (ed) (2011) *Ötzi 2.0. Eine Mumie zwischen Wissenschaft, Kult und Mythos.* Stuttgart

Gebühr, Michael (2009) *Moorleichen in Schleswig-Holstein.* Schleswig-Holstein

Georges, Patrice (2009) *Les momies, savoirs et représentations; de l'Égypte ancienne à Hollywood (Collection savoir et curiosités).* Paris

Germer, Renate (2010) *Mumien (Was ist was 84).* Nuremberg

Germer, Renate et al (eds) (2009) *Berliner Mumiengeschichten. Ergebnisse eines multidisziplinären Forschungsprojektes.* Regensburg

Geschichte und Tradition der Mumifizierung in Europa: Beiträge zu einer Tagung im Museum für Sepulkralkultur (2010) [publizierte

*Vorträge der Tagung "Geschichte und Tradition der
Mumifizierung in Europa].* Kassel 2011

Gill, A.A. (2009) *I morti viventi della Sicilia*, p94 – 109

Gill, A.A. (2009) 'Eine Siesta auf ewig', in: *National Geographic
Deutschland*, issue 2, p104 – 119

Gill-Frerking, Heathers, Rosendahl, Wilfried & Zink, Albert (eds)
(2011) *Yearbook of Mummy Studies 1*, Munich

Grilletto, Renato (2005) *Il mistero delle mummie: dall' antichità ai
nostri giorni attraverso il tempo e lo spazio (Universale storica
Newton 37).* Rome

Guidotti, Maria Cristina (2001) *Le mummie del Museo egizio di
Firenze (Maat 1).* Florence

Hansen, Jens Peder Hart, Meldgaard, Jørgen & Nordqvist, Jørgen
(eds) (1991) *The Greenland Mummies.* Washington D.C.

Hermann, Bernd & Meyer, Roelf-Diedrich (1993)
*Südamerikanische Mumien aus vorspanischer Zeit: eine
radiologische Untersuchung (Veröffentlichung des Museums für
Völkerkunde Berlin 58, Abteilung Amerikanische Archäologie 8).*
Berlin

Ikram, Salima (2003) *Death and Burial in Ancient Egypt.* London

Ikram, Salima & Dodson, Aidan (1998) *The Mummy in Ancient
Egypt: Equipping the Dead for Eternity.* London

Ikram, Salima & Iskander, Nasry (2002) *Non-human mummies
(Catalogue Général of Egyptian Antiquities in the Cairo Museum,
vols 24048 – 24056, 29504 – 29903 (selected), 51084 – 51101,
61089).* UK

*Imaging in mummiologia ed antropologia fisica: attia della giornata
di studio; Gradisca d'Isonzo, 15 gennaio 2007 (Quaderni di
bioarcheologia 1)* 2007

Janot, Francis (2008) *The Royal Mummies: Immortality in Ancient
Egypt* [Introduction by Zahi Hawass; Text by Francis Janot]. New York

Landesmuseum Baden-Württemberg (ed) (2007) *Ägyptische
Mumien: Unsterblichkeit im Land der Pharaonen (große
Landesausstellung Baden-Württemberg vom 6. Oktober 2007 bis
24. März 2008).* Mainz

*Le miroir du temps: les momies de Randazzo (Sicile, 17ᵉ – 19ᵉ s.);
exposition crée à St. Jean de Côle (Dordogne) en ouverture du 4e*

Colloque International de Pathographie; sous le Haut Patronage de M. Frédéric Mitterand, Ministre de la Culture et de la Communication (Collection Pathographie 7). Paris

Lohman, Jack & Goodnow, Katherine (eds) (2006) *Human Remains and Museum Practice (Museums and Diversity 918)*

Ludwig, Bigna (2008) *Mumien in Museen: Ethisch korrekter Umgang bei Konservierung/ Restaurierung, Lagerung und Ausstellung.* Saarbrücken

Lynnerup, Niels et al (eds) (2003) *Mummies in a New Millennium: Proceedings of the 4th World Congress on Mummy Studies. Nuuk, Greenland, September 4th to 10th 2001 (Danish Polar Center Publication 11).* Copenhagen

Maekawa, Shin (ed) (1998) *Oxygen-Free Museum Cases/ The Getty Conservation Institute (Research in Conservation).* Los Angeles

Malam, John (2003) *Mummies (Kingfisher Knowledge).* Boston

Mallory, James P. & Mair, Victor H. (2008) *The Tarim Mummies: Ancient China and the Mystery of the Earliest Peoples from the West.* London

Marinozzi, Silvia & Fornaciari, Gino (2005) *Le mummie e l'arte medica nell'evo moderno: per una storia dell'imbalsamazione artificiale dei corpi umani nell'evo moderno (Medicina nei secoli 17).* Rome

Mummies and Science: World Mummies Research: Proceedings of the VI World Congress on Mummy Studies (February 20th and 24th 2007). Teguise, Lanzarote 2008

Palao Pons, Pedro (2008) *Las momias del mundo (Misterio de la historia).* Arganda del Rey

Parra Ortiz, José Miguel (2010) *Momias: la derrota de la muerte en el antiguo Egipto (Tiempo de historia).* Barcelona

Partridge, Robert B. (1996) *Faces of Pharaohs: Royal Mummies and Coffins from Ancient Thebes.* Michigan

Pettigrew, Thomas Joseph (2009) *A History of Egyptian Mummies and an Account of the Worship and Embalming of the Sacred Animals by the Egyptians; with Remarks on the Funeral Ceremonies of Different Nations, and Observations on the Mummies of Canary Islands, of the Ancient Peruvians, Burman Priests, etc.* Charleston, SC

Picpican, Isikias (2003) *The Igorot Mummies: A Socio-Cultural and Historical Treatise.* Quezon City

Piombino-Mascali, Dario (2009) *Il maestro del sonno eterno. Presentazione di Arthur C. Aufderheide. Prefazione di Albert R. Zink (Le pietre 24).* Palermo

Pollès, Renan (2001) *La momie de Khéops à Hollywood: généalogie d'un mythe.* Paris

Pringle, Heather (2001) *The Mummy Congress: Science, Obsession, and the Everlasting Dead.* New York

Pusceddu, Raffaella (2009) *Gli ultimi imbalsamatori*, p110 – 113

Putnam, James & Hayman, Peter (1993) *Mumien. Das Geheimnis der konservierten Menschen- und Tierkörper (Sehen – Staunen – Wissen).* Hildesheim

Rabino Massa, Emma (ed) (2006) *World Congress on mummy studies 5, 2004, Torino: Proceedings/ V World Congress on Mummy Studies (Italy, 2nd - 5th September 2004), (Journal of Biological Research).* Turin

Raven, Maarten J. & Taconis, Wybren K. (eds) (2005) *Egyptian Mummies. Radiological Atlas of the Collections in the National Museum of Antiquities in Leiden (= Papers on Archaeology of the Leiden Museum of Antiquities, vol 1).* Turnhout

Reinhard, Johan (1998) *Discovering the Inca Ice Maiden. My Adventures on Ampato.* National Geographic Society, US

Reinhard, Johan (2005) *The Ice Maiden: Inca Mummies, Mountain Gods, and Sacred Sites in the Andes.* National Geographic Society, US

Roberts, Paul (2008) *Mummy Potraits from Roman Egypt.* London

Rose, Jerome C. (1997) *Bioarchaeology of Ancient Egypt and Nubia (British Museum Occasional Papers 112).* London

Sentinella, David E. (2007) *El enigma de las momias: claves históricas del arte de la momificación en las antiguas civilizaciones (Nowtilus frontera, Investigación abierta).* Madrid

Smith, Grafton Elliot & Dawson, Warren R. (2009) *Egyptian Mummies.* London

Smith, Grafton Elliot (2000) *The Royal Mummies (Catalogue général des antiquités égyptiennes du musée du Caire; vols 61051 – 61100. Service des antiquités de l'Égypte).* London

Spindler, Konrad et al (eds) (1996) *Human Mummies. A Global Survey of their Status and the Techniques of Conservation (The man in the ice 3).* Vienna & New York

Studies on Ancient Mummies and Burial Archaeology: Proceedings of the II World Congress on Mummy Studies held at the City of Cartagena de Indias (February of 1995). Columbia

Tanaka, Shelley (2005)*Mummies; The Newest, Coolest and Creepiest from around the World.* 3rd edition, New York

Tyson, Rose A. & Elerick, Daniel V. (eds) (1985) *Two Mummies from Chihuahua, Mexico: A Multidisciplinary Study (San Diego Museum Papers 19).* San Diego

Vockerodt, Gottfried (2009) *Mumiographica Medica. Oder Bericht von Egyptischen Mumien.* Whitefish (Montana)

Wang, Binghua (2002) *The Ancient Corpses of Xinjiang: The Peoples of Ancient Xinjiang and Their Culture.* Xinjiang

Wieczorek, Alfried (ed) (2007) *Mumien: Der Traum vom ewigen Leben; Begleitband zur Sonderausstellung "Mumien – Der Traum vom Ewigen Leben" in den Reiss-Engelhorn-Museen Mannheim vom 30. September 2007 bis 24. März 2008 (Publikationen der Reiss-Engelhorn-Museen 24).* Mannheim

Wolfe, S. J. & Singerman, Robert (2009) *Mummies in Nineteenth Century America: Ancient Egyptians as Artifacts.* Jefferson, NC

World Congress on Mummy Studies 1, 1992, Puerto de la Cruz (Actas del I Congreso Internacional de Estudios sobre Momias 1992). 2nd edition, 1995

Zink, Albert (2012) *From Tutankhamen to Ötzi: The Use of Modern Scientific Methods in Mummy Research (Kroon-Vordracht 34).* Amsterdam

Zink, Albert (2011) 'Konserviert für die Ewigkeit?', in: Angelika Fleckinger (ed): *Ötzi 2.0. Eine Mumie zwischen Wissenschaft, Kult und Mythos.* Stuttgart

Illustration Credits